INCREDIBLE AIR FRYER RECIPES

Publications International, Ltd.

Pictured on the front cover: (*clockwise from top left*): Oven "Fries" (*page 216*), Buttermilk Air-Fried Chicken (*page 109*), Air-Fried Parmesan Pickle Chips (*page 7*), Bacon-Roasted Brussels Sprouts (*page 204*), and Green Bean Fries (*page 200*).

Pictured on the back cover (*left to right*): Avocado Egg Rolls (*page 14*), Biscuit-Wrapped Sausages (*page 41*), and Chicken Air-Fried Steak with Creamy Gravy (*page 114*).

Several photographs and additional art on front cover copyright © Shutterstock.com. Photographs on pages 31 and 91 © Shutterstock.com.

Microwave Cooking: Microwave ovens vary in wattage. Use the cooking times as guidelines and check for doneness before adding more time.

Let's get social!
@Publications_International
@PublicationsInternational
www.pilcookbooks.com

CONTENTS

ENJOY YOUR AIR FRYER

Do you love fried foods but try to avoid them? You no longer need to worry.

The air fryer is your answer to preparing fried foods without the extra calories, fat, or mess in the kitchen. You'll get the taste, and texture of fried foods—crispy, tasty, and crunchy—that you love and crave, without the added guilt often felt when consuming them. Plus, you'll soon see how your air fryer is so easy to use, cooks food faster, and provides a no-fuss clean up.

You'll love the ability to prepare fried foods in your air fryer, but you'll also soon find that you can prepare all types of other foods, too. Make everything from appetizers to meals to sides and even desserts! Why not try cookies or muffins? What about trying marinated salmon or a tuna melt? You'll even love the taste of roasted vegetables. You can bake in it, grill in it, steam in it, roast in it, and reheat in it.

Choose from more than 120 ideas here, or create your own.

Now get started and have fun eating and serving all those healthier foods without the added guilt.

HELPFUL TIPS:

- Read your air fryer's manufacturer's directions carefully before cooking to make sure you understand the specific features of your air fryer before starting to cook.

- Preheat your air fryer for 2 to 3 minutes before cooking.

- You can cook foods typically prepared in the oven in your air fryer. But because the air fryer is more condensed than a regular oven, it is recommended that recipes cut 25°F to 50°F off temperature and 20% off the typical cooking times.

- Avoid having foods stick to your air fryer basket by using nonstick cooking spray or cooking on parchment paper or foil. You can also get food to brown and crisp more easily by spraying occasionally with nonstick cooking spray during the cooking process.

- Don't overfill your basket. Each air fryer differs in its basket size. Cook foods in batches as needed.

- Use toothpicks to hold food in place. You may notice that light foods may blow around from the pressure of the fan. Just be sure to secure foods in the basket to prevent this.

ENJOY YOUR AIR FRYER

- Check foods while cooking by opening the air fryer basket. This will not disturb cooking times. Once you return the basket, the cooking resumes.

- Experiment with cooking times of various foods. Test foods for doneness before consuming—check meats and poultry with a meat thermometer, and use a toothpick to test muffins and cupcakes.

- Use your air fryer to cook frozen foods, too! Frozen French fries, fish sticks, chicken nuggets, individual pizzas—these all work great. Just remember to reduce cooking temperatures and times.

ESTIMATED COOKING TEMPERATURES/TIMES*

FOOD	TEMPERATURE	TIMING
Vegetables (asparagus, broccoli, corn-on-the-cob, green beans, mushrooms, cherry tomatoes)	390°F	5 to 6 min.
Vegetables (bell peppers, cauliflower, eggplant, onions, potatoes, zucchini)	390°F	8 to 12 min.
Chicken (bone-in)	370°F	20 to 25 min.
Chicken (boneless)	370°F	12 to 15 min.
Beef (ground beef)	370°F	15 to 17 min.
Beef (steaks, roasts)	390°F	10 to 15 min.
Pork	370°F	12 to 15 min.
Fish	390°F	10 to 12 min.
Frozen Foods	390°F	10 to 15 min.

This is just a guide. All food varies in size, weight, and texture. Be sure to test your food for preferred doneness before consuming it. Also, some foods will need to be shaken or flipped to help distribute ingredients for proper cooking.

Make note of the temperatures and times that work best for you for continued success of your air fryer.

Enjoy and have fun!

APPEALING APPETIZERS

AIR-FRIED PARMESAN PICKLE CHIPS
MAKES 4 SERVINGS

4 large whole dill pickles
½ cup all-purpose flour
½ teaspoon salt
2 eggs

½ cup panko bread crumbs
2 tablespoons grated Parmesan cheese
½ cup garlic aoili mayonnaise or ranch dressing

1 Line baking sheet with paper towels. Slice pickles diagonally into ¼-inch slices, placing on prepared baking sheet. Pat dry on top with paper towels to remove any moisture from pickles.

2 Combine flour and salt in shallow dish. Beat eggs in another shallow dish. Combine panko and Parmesan cheese in third shallow dish.

3 Working assembly-line style, coat pickles in flour, dip in eggs, letting excess drip back into dish, then coat in panko.

4 Preheat air fryer to 390°F. Cook in batches 8 to 10 minutes or until golden brown. Remove carefully. Serve with aoili or dressing.

JALAPEÑO POPPERS
MAKES 20 TO 24 POPPERS

10 to 12 fresh jalapeño peppers*

1 package (8 ounces) cream cheese, softened

1½ cups (6 ounces) shredded Cheddar cheese, divided

2 green onions, finely chopped

½ teaspoon onion powder

¼ teaspoon salt

⅛ teaspoon garlic powder

6 slices bacon, crisp cooked and finely chopped

2 tablespoons panko bread crumbs

2 tablespoons grated Parmesan or Romano cheese

For large jalapeño peppers, use 10. For small peppers, use 12.

1 Cut each jalapeño pepper** in half lengthwise; remove ribs and seeds.

2 Combine cream cheese, 1 cup Cheddar cheese, green onions, onion powder, salt and garlic powder in medium bowl. Stir in bacon. Fill each pepper half with about 1 tablespoon cheese mixture. Sprinkle with remaining ½ cup Cheddar cheese, panko and Parmesan cheese.

3 Preheat air fryer to 370°F. Line basket with parchment paper or foil.

4 Cook 5 to 7 minutes or until cheese is melted and browned but peppers are still firm.

**Jalapeño peppers can sting and irritate the skin, so wear rubber gloves when handling peppers and do not touch your eyes.

LAVASH CHIPS WITH ARTICHOKE PESTO
MAKES 6 SERVINGS (ABOUT 1½ CUPS PESTO)

3 pieces lavash bread

¼ cup plus 2 tablespoons olive oil, divided

¾ teaspoon kosher salt, divided

1 can (14 ounces) artichoke hearts, rinsed and drained

½ cup chopped walnuts, toasted*

¼ cup packed fresh basil leaves

1 clove garlic, minced

2 tablespoons lemon juice

¼ cup grated Parmesan cheese

To toast nuts, cook in preheated 350°F parchment-lined air fryer 3 to 4 minutes until golden brown.

1 Preheat air fryer to 370°F. Line basket with parchment paper.

2 Brush both sides of lavash with 2 tablespoons oil. Sprinkle with ¼ teaspoon salt. Cut to fit in air fryer, if necessary. Cook in batches 8 to 10 minutes, shaking occasionally, until lavash is crisp and browned. Cool on wire rack.

3 Place artichoke hearts, walnuts, basil, garlic, lemon juice and remaining ½ teaspoon salt in food processor; pulse about 12 times until coarsely chopped. While food processor is running, slowly stream remaining ¼ cup oil until smooth. Add cheese and pulse until blended.

4 Serve lavash with pesto.

NOTE

You can also toast walnuts in preheated 350°F oven 6 to 8 minutes, if preferred.

CHEESY STUFFED MUSHROOMS
MAKES ABOUT 18 MUSHROOMS

4 ounces Brie, rind removed and cut into ½-inch cubes

8 ounces baby bella mushrooms, stems removed

½ cup seasoned dry bread crumbs

1 tablespoon fresh parsley leaves

2 tablespoons olive oil, divided

1 Preheat air fryer to 390°F.

2 Insert cube of cheese inside each mushroom cap. Stir bread crumbs, parsley and 1 tablespoon oil in small dish. Top each mushroom with bread crumb mixture. Brush with remaining oil.

3 Cook in batches 4 to 6 minutes or until topping is lightly browned.

TIP

Recipe can easily be doubled for a larger crowd.

AVOCADO EGG ROLLS
MAKES 10 SERVINGS

DIPPING SAUCE

- ½ **cup cashew nut pieces**
- ½ **cup packed fresh cilantro**
- ¼ **cup honey**
- 2 **green onions, coarsely chopped**
- 2 **cloves garlic**
- 1 **tablespoon white vinegar**
- 1 **teaspoon balsamic vinegar**
- 1 **teaspoon ground cumin**
- ½ **teaspoon tamarind paste**
- ⅛ **teaspoon ground turmeric**
- ¼ **cup olive oil**

EGG ROLLS

- 2 **avocados, peeled and pitted**
- ¼ **cup chopped drained oil-packed sun-dried tomatoes**
- 2 **tablespoons diced red onion**
- 2 **tablespoons chopped fresh cilantro**
- 1 **tablespoon lime juice**
- ¼ **teaspoon salt**
- 10 **egg roll wrappers**
- 1 **tablespoon vegetable oil**

1 For sauce, combine cashews, cilantro, honey, green onions, garlic, white vinegar, balsamic vinegar, cumin, tamarind paste and turmeric in food processor; process until coarsely chopped. With motor running, drizzle in olive oil in thin, steady stream; process until finely chopped and well blended. Refrigerate until ready to serve.

2 For egg rolls, place avocados in medium bowl; coarsely mash with potato masher. Stir in sun-dried tomatoes, red onion, chopped cilantro, lime juice and salt until well blended.

3 Working with one at a time, place egg roll wrapper on work surface with one corner facing you. Spread 2 tablespoons filling horizontally across wrapper. Fold short sides over filling and fold up bottom corner over filling. Moisten top edges with water; roll up egg roll, pressing to seal. Refrigerate until ready to cook.

4 Preheat air fryer to 390°F. Brush egg rolls with vegetable oil.

5 Cook in batches 6 to 8 minutes, turning once, until golden brown and crispy. Cut egg rolls in half diagonally; serve with sauce.

PEPPERONI BREAD
MAKES ABOUT 6 SERVINGS

1 package (about 14 ounces)
  refrigerated pizza dough

8 slices provolone cheese

20 to 30 slices pepperoni (about
  ½ of 6-ounce package)

¾ cup (3 ounces) shredded
  mozzarella cheese

½ cup grated Parmesan cheese

½ teaspoon Italian seasoning

1 egg, beaten

  Marinara sauce, heated

1 Preheat air fryer to 390°F. Line basket with parchment paper. Unroll pizza dough on lightly floured surface; cut dough in half.

2 Working with one half at a time, arrange half the provolone slices on half the dough. Top with half the pepperoni, half the mozzarella and Parmesan cheeses and half the Italian seasoning. Repeat with other half bread and toppings.

3 Fold top half of dough over filling; press edges with fork or pinch edges to seal. Transfer one bread to basket. Brush with egg.

4 Cook 8 to 10 minutes or until crust is golden brown. Remove to wire rack to cool slightly. Cool slightly. Repeat with other bread. Cut crosswise into slices; serve warm with marinara sauce.

CHEESE & SAUSAGE BUNDLES
MAKES 40 APPETIZERS

¼ **pound bulk hot Italian pork sausage**

1 **cup (4 ounces) shredded Monterey Jack cheese**

1 **can (4 ounces) diced mild green chiles, drained**

2 **tablespoons finely chopped green onion**

40 **wonton wrappers**

Prepared salsa

1 Brown sausage in small skillet over medium-high heat 6 to 8 minutes, stirring to break up meat. Drain off drippings.

2 Combine sausage, cheese, chiles and green onion in medium bowl. Spoon 1 round teaspoon sausage mixture near one corner of wonton wrapper. Brush opposite corner with water. Fold corner over filling; roll into cylinder.

3 Moisten ends of roll with water. Bring ends together to make a "bundle," overlapping ends slightly; firmly press to seal. Repeat with remaining filling and wonton wrappers.

4 Preheat air fryer to 370°F. Cook in batches 3 to 5 minutes or until golden brown. Serve with salsa.

MINI EGG ROLLS
MAKES 28 MINI EGG ROLLS

½ **pound ground pork**

3 **cloves garlic, minced**

1 **teaspoon minced fresh ginger**

¼ **teaspoon red pepper flakes**

6 **cups (12 ounces) shredded coleslaw mix**

¼ **cup reduced-sodium soy sauce**

1 **tablespoon cornstarch**

1 **tablespoon seasoned rice vinegar**

½ **cup chopped green onions**

28 **wonton wrappers**

Prepared sweet and sour sauce

Chinese hot mustard

1 Combine pork, garlic, ginger and red pepper flakes in large nonstick skillet; cook and stir over medium heat about 4 minutes or until pork is cooked through, stirring to break up meat. Add coleslaw mix; cover and cook 2 minutes. Uncover and cook 2 minutes or until coleslaw mix just begins to wilt.

2 Whisk soy sauce and cornstarch in small bowl until smooth and well blended; stir into pork mixture. Add vinegar; cook 2 to 3 minutes or until sauce is thickened. Remove from heat; stir in green onions.

3 Working with 1 wonton wrapper at a time, place wrapper on clean work surface. Spoon 1 level tablespoon pork mixture across and just below center of wrapper. Fold bottom point of wrapper up over filling; fold side points over filling, forming envelope shape. Moisten inside edges of top point with water and roll egg roll toward top point, pressing firmly to seal. Repeat with remaining wrappers and filling. Spray egg rolls with nonstick cooking spray.

4 Preheat air fryer to 370°F. Cook in batches 3 to 5 minutes until golden brown. Remove to cooling rack; cool slightly before serving. Serve with sweet and sour sauce and mustard for dipping.

GARLIC BITES
MAKES 24 TO 27 APPETIZERS

½ of 16-ounce package frozen phyllo dough, thawed to room temperature

¾ cup (1½ sticks) butter, melted

3 large heads garlic, separated into cloves, peeled

½ cup finely chopped walnuts

1 cup Italian-style bread crumbs

1 Remove phyllo from package; unroll and place on large sheet of waxed paper. Cut phyllo crosswise into 2-inch-wide strips. Cover phyllo with large sheet of plastic wrap and damp, clean kitchen towel. (Phyllo dries out quickly if not covered.)

2 Lay 1 strip of phyllo at a time on flat surface and brush immediately with butter. Place 1 clove of garlic at end. Sprinkle 1 teaspoon walnuts along length of strip.

3 Roll up garlic clove and walnuts in strip, tucking in side edges as you roll. Brush with butter; roll in bread crumbs. Repeat with remaining phyllo, garlic, walnuts, butter and bread crumbs.

4 Preheat air fryer to 350°F. Line basket with parchment paper. Cook in batches 6 to 8 minutes or until golden brown. Cool slightly.

HORS D'OEUVRE ROLLS
MAKES 40 ROLLS

½ cup Chinese-style thin egg noodles, broken into 1-inch pieces

2 tablespoons butter or margarine

4 ounces boneless lean pork, finely chopped

6 medium mushrooms, finely chopped

6 green onions with tops, finely chopped

8 ounces deveined shelled shrimp, cooked and finely chopped

1 hard-cooked egg, finely chopped

1½ tablespoons dry sherry

½ teaspoon salt

⅛ teaspoon black pepper

40 wonton wrappers

1 egg, lightly beaten

Prepared sweet and sour sauce

1 Cook noodles according to package directions; rinse and drain.

2 Heat butter in wok or large skillet over medium-high heat. Add pork; stir-fry about 5 minutes or until no longer pink in center. Add mushrooms and green onions; stir-fry 2 minutes.

3 Remove wok from heat. Add noodles, shrimp, hard-cooked egg, sherry, salt and pepper; mix well. Spoon 1 tablespoon pork mixture across center of each wonton wrapper. Brush edges lightly with beaten egg. Roll up tightly around filling; pinch edges slightly to seal.

4 Preheat air fryer to 370°F. Cook in batches 8 to 10 minutes, turning over halfway through cooking, until golden brown. Cool slightly. Serve with sweet and sour sauce.

TUNA ARTICHOKE CUPS

MAKES 12 APPETIZERS

1 can (5 ounces) tuna packed in water, preferably albacore, drained, liquid reserved

¼ cup minced shallots

1 tablespoon white wine vinegar

¼ teaspoon ground coriander

4 ounces cream cheese

1 can (14 ounces) artichoke hearts, drained and coarsely chopped

1 tablespoon lemon juice

½ teaspoon salt

¼ teaspoon white pepper

Dash ground nutmeg

12 wonton wrappers

2 tablespoons unsalted butter, melted

Chopped fresh parsley, toasted slivered almonds or chives (optional)

1 Combine reserved tuna liquid, shallots, vinegar and coriander in small saucepan over medium-high heat. Bring to a boil. Reduce heat; simmer, uncovered, until liquid has evaporated. Add tuna and cream cheese; cook, stirring constantly, until cheese melts. Stir in artichokes, lemon juice, salt, pepper and nutmeg. Cool slightly.

2 Gently press 1 wonton wrapper into 12 standard (2½-inch) silicone muffin cups, allowing ends to extend above edges of cups. Spoon about 1 tablespoon tuna mixture evenly into wonton wrappers. Brush edges of wonton wrappers with melted butter.

3 Preheat air fryer to 370°F. Cook 5 to 7 minutes or until tuna mixture is set and edges of wonton wrappers are browned. Garnish with parsley, almonds or chives.

MINI CHICKPEA CAKES
MAKES 2 DOZEN CAKES (ABOUT 8 SERVINGS)

1 can (about 15 ounces) chickpeas, rinsed and drained

1 cup grated carrots

⅓ cup seasoned dry bread crumbs

¼ cup creamy Italian salad dressing, plus additional for dipping

1 egg

1 Coarsely mash chickpeas in medium bowl with fork or potato masher. Stir in carrots, bread crumbs, ¼ cup salad dressing and egg; mix well.

2 Shape chickpea mixture into 24 patties, using about 1 tablespoon mixture for each.

3 Preheat air fryer to 370°F. Spray basket with nonstick cooking spray.

4 Cook in batches 10 minutes, turning halfway through cooking, until lightly browned. Serve warm with additional salad dressing for dipping, if desired.

THE BIG ONION
MAKES 6 SERVINGS

DIPPING SAUCE
- ½ **cup light mayonnaise**
- 2 **tablespoons horseradish**
- 1 **tablespoon ketchup**
- ¼ **teaspoon paprika**
- ⅛ **teaspoon salt**
- ⅛ **teaspoon ground red pepper**
- ⅛ **teaspoon dried oregano**

ONION
- 1 **large sweet onion (about 1 pound)**
- ½ **cup all-purpose flour**
- 1 **tablespoon buttermilk**
- 2 **eggs**
- ½ **cup panko bread crumbs**
- 1 **tablespoon paprika**
- 1½ **teaspoons seafood seasoning**

1 For sauce, combine mayonnaise, horseradish, ketchup, ¼ teaspoon paprika, salt, ground red pepper and oregano in small bowl; mix well. Cover and refrigerate until ready to serve.

2 For onion, cut about ½ inch off top of onion and peel off papery skin. Place onion cut side down on cutting board. Starting ½ inch from root, use large sharp knife to make one slice down to cutting board. Repeat slicing all the way around onion to make 12 to 16 evenly spaced cuts. Turn onion over; gently separate outer pieces.

3 Meanwhile, put flour in large bowl. Whisk buttermilk and eggs in another large bowl. Combine panko, 1 tablespoon paprika and seafood seasoning in another bowl.

4 Coat onion with flour, shaking off any excess. Dip entire onion in egg mixture, letting excess drip back into bowl. Then coat evenly with panko.

5 Preheat air fryer to 390°F. Spray basket with nonstick cooking spray.

6 Cook 10 to 12 minutes or until golden brown and crispy. Serve immediately with dipping sauce.

CHILI PUFFS
MAKES 9 PUFFS

1 **sheet puff pastry (half of 17¼-ounce package), thawed**

1 **can (about 15 ounces) chili without beans**

1 **package (about 4 ounces) cream cheese, softened**

¼ **cup (1 ounce) finely shredded sharp Cheddar cheese**

Sliced green onions (optional)

1 Spray 2½-inch silicone muffin cups with nonstick cooking spray.

2 Roll out puff pastry on lightly floured surface. Cut nine 3-inch squares. Press dough into muffin cups.

3 Preheat air fryer to 390°F. Cook in batches 6 to 8 minutes or until golden brown. Cool slightly.

4 Meanwhile, combine chili and cream cheese in small saucepan over medium-low heat. Heat until warmed, stirring occasionally, until cream cheese blends into chili mixture. Remove from heat.

5 Fill each pastry shell with 2 teaspoons chili mixture, pressing down centers of pastry to fill, if necessary. Sprinkle evenly with Cheddar cheese. Garnish with green onions, if desired.

TIP

Use a pizza cutter to easily cut puff pastry sheets.

FISH BITES WITH ROMESCO SAUCE
MAKES 4 SERVINGS

1 jar (12 ounces) roasted red peppers, drained

4 plum tomatoes, quartered

½ cup raw almonds

2 cloves garlic, peeled

¼ cup fresh parsley leaves

1 tablespoon olive oil

1 tablespoon lemon juice

½ teaspoon salt, divided

2 egg whites

¼ cup all-purpose flour

½ teaspoon ground red pepper

¼ cup ground almonds

½ pound tilapia fillets, cut into 1-inch pieces

1 For sauce, place roasted red peppers, tomatoes, almonds, garlic, parsley, oil, lemon juice and ¼ teaspoon salt in food processor; process using on/off pulsing action just until ingredients are almost smooth. Place sauce in small bowl; set aside.

2 Lightly beat egg whites in small bowl. Combine flour, ground red pepper and remaining ¼ teaspoon salt in shallow dish. Place ground almonds in second shallow dish.

3 Coat fish in flour mixture, shaking off excess. Dip into egg whites; roll in ground almonds until evenly coated.

4 Preheat air fryer to 390°F. Lightly spray basket with nonstick cooking spray.

5 Cook in batches 8 to 10 minutes or until golden brown and fish begins to flake when tested with fork. Serve immediately with sauce.

TURKEY MEATBALLS WITH YOGURT-CUCUMBER SAUCE
MAKES 30 MEATBALLS

1 pound lean ground turkey or chicken

1 cup finely chopped onion

½ cup plain dry bread crumbs

¼ cup whipping cream

2 cloves garlic, minced

1 egg, lightly beaten

3 tablespoons chopped fresh mint

1 teaspoon salt

¼ teaspoon ground red pepper

1 tablespoon olive oil

Yogurt-Cucumber Sauce (recipe follows)

1 Combine turkey, onion, bread crumbs, cream, garlic, egg, mint, salt and ground red pepper in large bowl; mix well. Shape into 30 meatballs. Place meatballs on baking sheet. Cover with plastic wrap; refrigerate 1 hour.

2 Preheat air fryer to 390°F. Line basket with parchment paper; spray with nonstick cooking spray.

3 Brush meatballs with oil. Cook in batches 12 to 14 minutes, shaking halfway through cooking, until cooked through.

4 Meanwhile, prepare Yogurt-Cucumber Sauce. Serve meatballs with sauce.

YOGURT-CUCUMBER SAUCE
MAKES ABOUT 1 CUP

1 container (6 ounces) plain nonfat Greek yogurt

½ cup peeled seeded and finely chopped cucumber

2 teaspoons chopped fresh mint

2 teaspoons grated lemon peel

2 teaspoons lemon juice

¼ teaspoon salt

Combine all ingredients in small bowl. Refrigerate until ready to serve.

BAKED SALAMI
MAKES 5 SERVINGS

1 all-beef kosher salami
(14 to 16 ounces)

½ cup apricot preserves

1 tablespoon hot pepper sauce

2 tablespoons packed brown
sugar

Bread slices

1 Peel off plastic wrap of salami. Cut 12 crosswise (½-inch-deep) slits across top. Place, cut side up, in small dish that fits inside air fryer.

2 Combine preserves, hot pepper sauce and brown sugar in small bowl; stir well. Spoon sauce over top.

3 Preheat air fryer to 370°F. Cook 8 to 10 minutes or until juicy and dark brown, spooning sauce over salami occasionally during cooking.

4 Cut salami into thin slices; toss with sauce. Serve on bread.

EXTRAS
Serve with slices of challah bread or cocktail rye.

BREAKFAST BITES

BISCUIT-WRAPPED SAUSAGES
MAKES 6 SERVINGS

½ can (8-count) refrigerated
biscuit dough

1 package (about 12 ounces) fully
cooked breakfast sausage

Maple syrup (optional)

1 Cut 3 biscuits into four pieces; roll each piece into 2-inch rope. Wrap each sausage with dough. Insert wooden skewers* through sausages.

2 Preheat air fryer to 370°F.

3 Cook 5 to 7 minutes or until golden brown. Cool slightly; remove to large serving platter. Serve with maple syrup for dipping.

*Soak wooden skewers 20 minutes in cool water. Depending on the size of your air fryer, you may need to shorten the skewers to fit.

BREAKFAST BURRITOS
MAKES 4 SERVINGS

4 turkey breakfast sausage links

2 eggs

½ teaspoon ground cumin (optional)

4 (6-inch) yellow or white corn tortillas

¼ cup prepared salsa

1 Preheat air fryer to 370°F. Line basket with parchment paper.

2 Cook sausages 6 to 8 minutes or until browned on the outside and cooked through, shaking occasionally during cooking. Remove sausages to plate.

3 Whisk eggs and cumin, if desired, in small bowl. Heat small skillet over medium-high heat. Cook eggs until done.

4 Place sausage link in middle of each tortilla. Spoon equal amounts of scrambled egg on top of sausage. Roll up to enclose the filling; secure with toothpicks.

5 Cook in air fryer 2 to 3 minutes or until heated through.

6 Pour salsa in small bowl. Serve with burritos.

SWEET BREAKFAST TACOS

Substitute four 4-inch frozen pancakes for the tortillas and ¼ cup light maple syrup for the salsa. Stack pancakes on microwavable plate. Microwave on HIGH 30 to 60 seconds or until warmed through. To assemble tacos, place pancake on flat surface. Place sausage link in middle of pancake. Spoon 2 tablespoons egg along length of sausage. Fold in half. Repeat with the remaining pancakes, sausages, and scrambled egg. Pour maple syrup into small bowl. Serve on the side for dipping or for drizzling over tacos.

BISCUIT DOUGHNUTS
MAKES 8 DOUGHNUTS

1 package (about 16 ounces) refrigerated jumbo biscuit dough (8 biscuits)

¼ cup honey

1 teaspoon chopped pistachio nuts

1 Separate dough into eight portions. Using hands, create a hole in the middle to create doughnut shape.

2 Preheat air fryer to 370°F.

3 Cook in batches 7 to 8 minutes or until golden brown.

4 Drizzle warm doughnuts with honey. Sprinkle with pistachios.

VARIATION

For cinnamon-sugar coating, combine ¼ cup sugar and 1 teaspoon ground cinnamon in small bowl. Dip warm doughnuts in cinnamon-sugar topping.

EASY RASPBERRY-PEACH DANISH

MAKES 8 SERVINGS

1 **package (8 ounces) refrigerated crescent dough sheet**

¼ **cup raspberry fruit spread**

1 **can (about 15 ounces) sliced peaches in juice, drained and chopped**

1 **egg white, beaten**

½ **cup powdered sugar**

2 **to 3 teaspoons orange juice**

¼ **cup chopped pecans, toasted***

*To toast nuts, cook in preheated 350°F parchment-lined air fryer 3 to 4 minutes until golden brown.

1 Place dough on lightly floured surface; cut in half. Roll each half into 12×8-inch rectangle.

2 Spread half of raspberry spread along center of each dough rectangle; top with peaches. Make 2-inch-long cuts from edges towards filling on long sides of each dough rectangle at 1-inch intervals. Fold strips of dough over filling. Brush with egg white.

3 Preheat air fryer to 370°F. Line basket with parchment paper. Cook each half 5 to 7 minutes or until golden brown. Remove to wire rack; cool slightly.

4 Combine powdered sugar and enough orange juice in small bowl to make pourable glaze. Drizzle glaze over Danish; sprinkle with pecans.

BREAKFAST PEPPERONI FLATBREAD
MAKES 2 SERVINGS

1 flatbread

½ cup (2 ounces) shredded mozzarella cheese

1 plum tomato, diced

12 slices turkey pepperoni, cut into quarters

1 teaspoon grated Parmesan cheese

¼ cup chopped fresh basil

1 Preheat air fryer to 370°F. Place flatbread on parchment paper. Sprinkle with mozzarella cheese, tomatoes, pepperoni and Parmesan cheese.

2 Cook 3 to 5 minutes or until cheese is melted. Sprinkle with basil. Cool slightly before cutting.

RASPBERRY WHITE CHOCOLATE DANISH
MAKES 8 SERVINGS

1 package (8 ounces) refrigerated crescent roll dough

8 teaspoons red raspberry preserves

1 ounce white baking chocolate, chopped

1 Unroll crescent dough; separate into eight triangles. Place 1 teaspoon preserves in center of each triangle. Fold right and left corners of long side over filling to top corner to form rectangle. Pinch edges to seal.

2 Preheat air fryer to 370°F. Line basket with parchment paper; spray with nonstick cooking spray.

3 Cook, seam side up, in batches 5 to 7 minutes or until lightly browned. Remove to wire rack to cool 5 minutes.

4 Place white chocolate in small resealable food storage bag. Microwave on MEDIUM (50%) 1 minute; gently knead bag. Microwave and knead at additional 30-second intervals until chocolate is completely melted. Cut off small corner of bag; drizzle chocolate over danish.

CINNAMINI BUNS
MAKES 2 DOZEN

2 **tablespoons packed brown sugar**

½ **teaspoon ground cinnamon**

1 **package (8 ounces) refrigerated crescent roll dough**

1 **tablespoon butter, melted**

½ **cup powdered sugar**

1 **to 1½ tablespoons milk**

1 Combine brown sugar and cinnamon in small bowl; mix well.

2 Unroll dough and separate into two 12×4-inch rectangles; firmly press perforations to seal. Brush dough with melted butter; sprinkle with brown sugar mixture. Starting with long side, roll up tightly jelly-roll style; pinch seams to seal. Cut each roll crosswise into 12 (1-inch) slices with serrated knife.

3 Preheat air fryer to 370°F. Line basket with parchment paper.

4 Cook, seam side up, in batches 5 to 7 minutes or until golden brown. Remove to wire rack; cool.

5 Combine powdered sugar and 1 tablespoon milk in small bowl; whisk until smooth. Add additional milk, 1 teaspoon at a time, to reach desired glaze consistency. Drizzle glaze over buns.

PEANUT BUTTER AND JELLY FRENCH TOAST
MAKES 6 SERVINGS

1 banana, sliced

2 tablespoons peanuts, chopped

2 tablespoons orange juice

1 tablespoon honey

6 slices whole wheat bread

¼ cup grape jelly (or favorite flavor)

¼ cup peanut butter

2 eggs

¼ cup milk

1 Combine banana, peanuts, orange juice and honey in small bowl; set aside. Spread 3 bread slices with jelly and 3 slices with peanut butter. Press peanut butter and jelly slices together to form 3 sandwiches; cut each sandwich in half diagonally.

2 Beat eggs and milk in shallow dish. Dip sandwiches in egg mixture, turning to coat.

3 Preheat air fryer to 350°F. Line basket with parchment paper.

4 Cook in batches 3 to 4 minutes per side or until light golden brown. Top with banana mixture.

APPLE BUTTER ROLLS
MAKES 12 SERVINGS

1 package (about 11 ounces) refrigerated breadstick dough (12 breadsticks)

2 tablespoons apple butter

¼ cup sifted powdered sugar

1 to 1½ teaspoons orange juice

¼ teaspoon grated orange peel (optional)

1 Unroll breadstick dough; separate into 12 pieces along perforations. Gently stretch each piece to 9 inches in length. Twist ends of each piece in opposite directions three or four times. Coil each twisted strip into snail shape; tuck ends underneath. Use thumb to make small indentation in center of each breadstick coil. Spoon about ½ teaspoon apple butter into each indentation.

2 Preheat air fryer to 370°F. Line basket with parchment paper; spray with nonstick cooking spray.

3 Cook in batches 8 to 10 minutes or until golden brown. Remove to wire rack; cool 10 minutes.

4 Meanwhile, combine powdered sugar and 1 teaspoon orange juice in small bowl; whisk until smooth. Add additional orange juice, if necessary, to make pourable glaze. Stir in orange peel, if desired. Drizzle glaze over rolls. Serve warm.

BISCUIT BREAKFAST PIZZAS
MAKES 8 SERVINGS

1 package (about 16 ounces) refrigerated flaky biscuit dough

8 tablespoons tomato sauce

2 slices turkey bacon

¼ cup chopped green bell pepper (optional)

¼ cup chopped onion (optional)

1¼ cups egg substitute

¼ teaspoon black pepper

½ cup (2 ounces) shredded Cheddar cheese

1 Separate biscuits. Make indentation in center of each biscuit. Spoon 1 tablespoon tomato sauce into center.

2 Cook bacon, bell pepper and onion, if desired, in large nonstick skillet over medium-high heat until crisp. Remove bacon to paper towels. Drain drippings from skillet.

3 Spray same skillet with nonstick cooking spray. Add egg substitute; season with black pepper. Cook about 1 minute, stirring often, until eggs are set.

4 Spoon eggs evenly into biscuit centers. Crumble bacon; sprinkle over eggs. Top with cheese.

5 Preheat air fryer to 370°F. Cook in batches 6 to 8 minutes or until pizza edges are golden brown.

VARIATION

Try substituting low-fat sausage for the bacon in this recipe. Or, try another of your favorite reduced-fat cheeses in place of the Cheddar.

BREAKFAST EMPANADAS
MAKES 4 SERVINGS

1 package (15 ounces) refrigerated pie crusts (2 crusts)

9 eggs, divided

1 teaspoon water

1 teaspoon salt

Dash black pepper

1 tablespoon butter

½ pound bacon (about 10 slices), crisp-cooked and cut into ¼-inch pieces

2 cups (8 ounces) Mexican-style shredded cheese, divided

4 tablespoons prepared salsa

1 Place pie crusts on flat surface; cut into halves to make four semicircles.

2 Beat 1 egg and water in small bowl until well blended; set aside. Beat remaining 8 eggs, salt and pepper in medium bowl until well blended. Heat large skillet over medium heat. Add butter; tilt skillet to coat bottom. Sprinkle bacon evenly in skillet. Pour eggs into skillet; cook 2 minutes without stirring. Gently start stirring until eggs form large curds and are still slightly moist. Transfer to plate to cool.

3 Spoon one fourth of cooled scrambled egg mixture onto half of each pie crust. Reserve ¼ cup cheese; sprinkle remaining cheese evenly over eggs. Top with salsa.

4 Brush inside edges of each semicircle with reserved egg-water mixture. Fold dough over top of egg mixture and seal edges with fork. (Flour fork tines to prevent sticking, if necessary.) Brush tops of empanadas with remaining egg-water mixture; sprinkle with reserved ¼ cup cheese.

5 Preheat air fryer to 370°F. Spray basket with nonstick cooking spray.

6 Cook in batches in air fryer 10 to 12 minutes or until golden.

TIP

These make a great main dish for dinner, too. Plus, they can be prepared early in the day and reheated in a preheated 350°F oven for 20 to 25 minutes.

MINI ASPARAGUS QUICHES
MAKES 10 SERVINGS

3 **to 4 stalks asparagus**
3 **eggs**
¼ **teaspoon salt**

¼ **teaspoon black pepper**
1 **unbaked 9-inch pie crust**

1 LIghtly spray 1¾-inch silicone muffin cups with nonstick cooking spray.

2 Trim asparagus; thinly slice on the diagonal or coarsely chop enough to make ¼ cup. Bring 1½ cups water to a boil in medium saucepan. Add asparagus; cook 2 minutes over medium heat. Drain in colander; rinse under cold water.

3 Whisk eggs, salt and pepper in medium bowl; stir in asparagus.

4 Roll out pie dough into 13-inch circle. Cut out circles with 3-inch round biscuit cutter. Gather and reroll scraps to make 20 circles. Press circles into silicone muffin cups. Fill cups with egg mixture.

5 Preheat air fryer to 370°F. Cook in batches 8 to 10 minutes or until tops are lightly browned and toothpick inserted into centers comes out clean.

VARIATION

Mini Swiss Quiches: Prepare the muffin cups as directed, then whisk together 4 eggs, ¼ teaspoon salt and ¼ teaspoon black pepper. Stir in ¾ cup shredded Swiss cheese. Make dough circles as directed, and fill cups with egg mixture. Cook as directed. Makes 20 mini quiches.

NO-FUSS LUNCH

SPINACH & ROASTED PEPPER PANINI
MAKES 4 SERVINGS

1 loaf (12 ounces) focaccia

1½ cups spinach leaves (about 12 leaves)

1 jar (about 7 ounces) roasted red peppers, drained

4 ounces fontina cheese, thinly sliced

¾ cup thinly sliced red onion

Olive oil

1 Cut focaccia in half horizontally. Layer bottom half with spinach, peppers, cheese and onion. Cover with top half of focaccia. Brush outsides of sandwich lightly with oil. Cut sandwich into 4 equal pieces.

2 Preheat air fryer to 370°F. Line basket with parchment paper. Cook in batches 3 to 5 minutes or until cheese melts and bread is golden brown.

NOTE

Focaccia can be found in the bakery section of most supermarkets. It is often available in different flavors, such as tomato, herb, cheese or onion.

JAPANESE FRIED CHICKEN ON WATERCRESS

MAKES 4 SERVINGS

1 pound boneless skinless chicken breasts, cut into 2-inch pieces

3 tablespoons tamari or soy sauce

2 tablespoons sake

3 cloves garlic, minced

1 teaspoon minced fresh ginger

⅓ cup cornstarch

3 tablespoons all-purpose flour

SALAD

¼ cup unseasoned rice vinegar

3 teaspoons tamari or soy sauce

1 teaspoon dark sesame oil

2 bunches watercress, trimmed of tough stems

1 pint grape tomatoes, halved

1 Place chicken in large resealable food storage bag. Mix 3 tablespoons tamari, sake, garlic and ginger in small bowl. Pour over chicken and marinate in refrigerator at least 30 minutes, turning bag occasionally.

2 Combine cornstarch and flour in shallow dish. Drain chicken and discard marinade. Roll chicken pieces in cornstarch mixture and shake off excess.

3 Preheat air fryer to 370°F. Cook in batches 8 to 10 minutes or until chicken is golden brown.

4 For salad, whisk together vinegar, 3 teaspoons tamari and sesame oil in small bowl. Arrange watercress and tomatoes on serving plates. Drizzle with dressing and top with chicken.

TUNA MELTS
MAKES 2 SERVINGS

1 can (about 5 ounces) chunk white tuna packed in water, drained and flaked

½ cup packaged coleslaw mix

1 tablespoon sliced green onion

1 tablespoon mayonnaise

½ tablespoon Dijon mustard

¼ teaspoon dried dill weed (optional)

2 English muffins, split

¼ cup (1 ounce) shredded Cheddar cheese

1 Combine tuna, coleslaw mix and green onion in medium bowl. Combine mayonnaise, mustard and dill weed, if desired, in small bowl. Stir mayonnaise mixture into tuna mixture. Spread tuna mixture onto muffin halves.

2 Preheat air fryer to 370°F. Cook 3 to 4 minutes or until heated through and lightly browned. Sprinkle with cheese. Cook 1 to 2 minutes until cheese melts.

BELL PEPPER AND RICOTTA CALZONES
MAKES 6 SERVINGS

2 teaspoons olive oil

1 medium red bell pepper, diced

1 medium green bell pepper, diced

1 small onion, diced

½ teaspoon Italian seasoning

⅛ teaspoon black pepper

1 clove garlic, minced

1¼ cups marinara sauce, divided

¼ cup ricotta cheese

⅛ cup mozzarella cheese

1 package (14 ounces) refrigerated pizza dough

1 Heat oil in medium nonstick skillet over medium heat. Add bell peppers, onion, Italian seasoning and black pepper. Cook about 8 minutes, stirring occasionally until vegetables are tender. Add garlic, and cook, stirring constantly, 1 minute. Stir in ½ cup marinara sauce; cook about 2 minutes until thickened slightly. Transfer vegetable mixture to plate; let cool slightly.

2 Combine ricotta cheese and mozzarella cheese in small bowl. Unroll pizza dough and cut into six 4×4-inch squares. Pat each square into 5×5-inch square. Spoon ⅓ cup vegetable mixture into center of each square. Top vegetables with 1 tablespoon cheese mixture. Fold dough over filling to form triangle; pinch and fold edges together to seal.

3 Preheat air fryer to 370°F. Line basket with parchment paper.

4 Cook in batches 8 to 10 minutes or until lightly browned. Cool 5 minutes. Serve with remaining marinara sauce.

STUFFED PARTY BAGUETTE
MAKES 12 SERVINGS

2 medium red bell peppers

1 loaf French bread (about 14 inches long)

¼ cup plus 2 tablespoons Italian dressing, divided

1 small red onion, very thinly sliced

8 large fresh basil leaves

3 ounces Swiss cheese, very thinly sliced

1 Preheat air fryer to 390°F.

2 To roast bell peppers, cut in half; remove stems, seeds and membranes. Place peppers, cut sides down, in basket. Cook 15 minutes, turning once or twice. When done cooking, let sit in basket 10 minutes before removing.

3 Use paring knife to carefully remove skin. (It should easily come off.) Discard skins; cut peppers into strips.

4 Trim ends from bread. Cut loaf in half lengthwise. Remove soft insides of loaf; reserve for another use.

5 Brush ¼ cup Italian dressing evenly onto cut sides of bread. Arrange pepper strips on bottom half of loaf; top with onion. Brush onion with remaining 2 tablespoons Italian dressing; top with basil and cheese. Replace bread top. Wrap loaf tightly in plastic wrap; refrigerate at least 2 hours.

6 To serve, remove plastic wrap. Cut loaf crosswise into slices. Secure with toothpicks.

BEEF AND BEER SLIDERS
MAKES 12 SLIDERS

6 tablespoons ketchup

2 tablespoons mayonnaise

2 teaspoons Dijon mustard

1½ pounds ground beef

½ cup beer

1 teaspoon salt

½ teaspoon garlic powder

½ teaspoon onion powder

½ teaspoon ground cumin

½ teaspoon dried oregano

¼ teaspoon black pepper

3 slices sharp Cheddar cheese, each cut into 4 pieces

12 slider buns or potato dinner rolls

12 baby lettuce leaves

12 plum tomato slices

1 Combine ketchup, mayonnaise and mustard in small bowl; reserve.

2 Combine beef, beer, salt, garlic powder, onion powder, cumin, oregano and pepper in medium bowl. Shape mixture into 12 (¼-inch-thick) patties.

3 Preheat air fryer to 370°F. Spray basket with nonstick cooking spray. Cook patties in batches 5 to 6 minutes; turn over. Top each patty with 1 piece cheese. Cook in batches 5 to 6 minutes or until cheese is melted and patties are cooked through. Remove to large plate; keep warm.

4 Serve sliders on rolls with ketchup mixture, lettuce and tomato.

MOZZARELLA & ROASTED RED PEPPER SANDWICH
MAKES 1 SANDWICH

1 tablespoon olive oil vinaigrette or Italian salad dressing

2 slices Italian-style sandwich bread (2 ounces)

2 fresh basil leaves

⅓ cup roasted red peppers, rinsed, drained and patted dry

1 to 2 slices (1 ounce each) part-skim mozzarella or Swiss cheese

1 Brush dressing on 1 side of 1 bread slice; top with basil, roasted peppers, cheese and remaining bread slice. Lightly spray both sides of sandwich with nonstick cooking spray.

2 Preheat air fryer to 350°F. Cook 4 to 5 minutes, turning halfway through cooking, until cheese melts and bread is golden brown.

SPICY EGGPLANT BURGERS
MAKES 4 SERVINGS

1 **eggplant (about 1¼ pounds)**

2 **egg whites**

½ **cup Italian-style panko bread crumbs**

3 **tablespoons chipotle mayonnaise or regular mayonnaise**

4 **whole wheat hamburger buns, warmed**

1½ **cups loosely packed baby spinach**

8 **thin slices tomato**

4 **slices pepper jack cheese**

1 Cut four ½-inch-thick slices from widest part of eggplant. Beat egg whites in shallow bowl. Place panko on medium plate.

2 Dip eggplant slices in egg whites; dredge in panko, pressing gently to adhere. Spray with nonstick cooking spray.

3 Preheat air fryer to 370°F. Line basket with foil. Cook in batches 6 to 8 minutes on each side or until golden brown.

4 Spread mayonnaise on bottom halves of buns; top with spinach, tomatoes, eggplant, cheese and tops of buns.

BUFFALO CHICKEN WRAPS

MAKES 2 SERVINGS

- 2 **boneless skinless chicken breasts (about 4 ounces each)**
- 4 **tablespoons buffalo wing sauce, divided**
- 1 **cup broccoli slaw**
- 1½ **teaspoons light blue cheese salad dressing**
- 2 **(8-inch) whole wheat tortillas, warmed**

1 Place chicken in large resealable food storage bag. Add 2 tablespoons buffalo sauce; seal bag. Marinate in refrigerator 15 minutes.

2 Preheat air fryer to 370°F. Cook 8 to 10 minutes per side or until no longer pink in center. When cool enough to handle, slice chicken; combine with remaining 2 tablespoons buffalo sauce in medium bowl.

3 Combine broccoli slaw and blue cheese dressing in medium bowl; mix well.

4 Arrange chicken and broccoli slaw evenly down center of each tortilla. Roll up to secure filling. To serve, cut in half diagonally.

TIP

If you do not like the spicy flavor of buffalo wing sauce, substitute your favorite barbecue sauce.

SOUTHWESTERN CHILI CHEESE EMPANADAS
MAKES 6 TO 8 SERVINGS

¾ **cup (3 ounces) finely shredded taco-flavored cheese***

⅓ **cup diced green chiles, drained**

1 **package (15 ounces) refrigerated pie crusts (2 crusts)**

1 **egg**

1 **tablespoon water**

Chili powder

*If taco-flavored cheese is unavailable, toss ¾ cup shredded Colby Jack cheese with ½ teaspoon chili powder.

1 Combine cheese and chiles in small bowl.

2 Unfold 1 pastry crust on floured surface. Roll into 13-inch circle. Cut dough rounds using 3-inch cookie cutter, rerolling scraps as necessary. Repeat with remaining crust.

3 Spoon 1 teaspoon cheese mixture in center of each dough round. Fold round in half, sealing edge with tines of fork.

4 Place empanadas on waxed paper-lined baking sheets; freeze, uncovered, 1 hour or until firm. Place in resealable food storage bags. Freeze up to 2 months, if desired.

5 To complete recipe, preheat air fryer to 370°F. Beat egg and water in small bowl; brush on empanadas. Sprinkle with chili powder.

6 Cook in batches 8 to 10 minutes or until golden brown. Remove to wire rack to cool.

SERVING SUGGESTION

Serve empanadas with salsa and sour cream.

PIZZA SANDWICH
MAKES 4 TO 6 SERVINGS

1 loaf (12 ounces) focaccia

½ cup pizza sauce

20 slices pepperoni

8 slices (1 ounce each) mozzarella cheese

1 can (2¼ ounces) sliced mushrooms, drained

Red pepper flakes (optional)

Olive oil

1 Cut focaccia horizontally in half. Spread cut sides of both halves with pizza sauce. Layer bottom half with pepperoni, cheese and mushrooms; sprinkle with red pepper flakes, if desired. Cover with top half of focaccia. Brush sandwich lightly with oil.*

2 Preheat air fryer to 370°F.

3 Cook 3 to 5 minutes or until cheese melts and bread is golden brown. Cut into wedges to serve.

Depending on the size of your air fryer, you may need to cut the focaccia vertically in half to fit.

NOTE

Focaccia can be found in the bakery section of most supermarkets. It is often available in different flavors, such as tomato, herb, cheese or onion.

CHESAPEAKE CRAB CAKES
MAKES 6 SERVINGS

1 pound backfin crabmeat

½ cup fresh bread crumbs

1 tablespoon minced onion

1 tablespoon finely chopped green bell pepper

1 tablespoon chopped fresh parsley

¼ cup mayonnaise

1 egg

2 teaspoons white wine Worcestershire sauce

2 teaspoons lemon juice

1 teaspoon prepared mustard

½ teaspoon salt

¼ teaspoon white pepper

Prepared tartar sauce

1 Pick out and discard any shell or cartilage from crabmeat. Flake with fork. Place crabmeat in medium bowl. Add bread crumbs, onion, bell pepper and parsley; set aside.

2 Mix remaining ingredients except tartar sauce in medium bowl. Stir well to combine. Pour mayonnaise mixture over crabmeat mixture. Gently mix so large lumps will not be broken. Shape mixture into six cakes. Place on baking sheet; refrigerate 15 to 20 minutes or until firm.

3 Preheat air fryer to 350°F. Spray basket with nonstick cooking spray.

4 Cook in batches 8 to 10 minutes or until lightly browned.

5 Serve with tartar sauce.

SIMPLE SNACKS

EVERYTHING SEASONING DIP WITH BAGEL CHIPS

MAKES ABOUT 2 CUPS DIP

2 large bagels, sliced vertically into rounds

1 container (12 ounces) whipped cream cheese

1½ tablespoons green onion tops, chopped

1 teaspoon minced onion

1 teaspoon minced garlic

1 teaspoon sesame seeds

1 teaspoon poppy seeds

¼ teaspoon kosher salt

1 Preheat air fryer to 350°F.

2 Coat bagel rounds generously with butter-flavored cooking spray. Cook 7 to 8 minutes until golden brown, shaking occasionally.

3 Combine cream cheese, green onion, minced onion, garlic, sesame seeds, poppy seeds and salt in medium bowl; stir to blend.

4 Serve chips with dip.

CORN TORTILLA CHIPS
MAKES 6 DOZEN CHIPS (12 SERVINGS)

6 (6-inch) corn tortillas, preferably day-old

½ teaspoon salt

Prepared guacamole or salsa

1 If tortillas are fresh, let stand, uncovered, in single layer on wire rack 1 to 2 hours to dry slightly.

2 Stack tortillas; cut tortillas into 6 or 8 equal wedges. Spray tortillas generously with nonstick olive oil cooking spray.

3 Preheat air fryer to 370°F.

4 Cook in batches 5 to 6 minutes, shaking halfway through cooking. Sprinkle with salt. Serve with guacamole or salsa, if desired.

NOTE

Tortilla chips are served with salsa as a snack, used as the base for nachos and used as scoops for guacamole, other dips or refried beans. They are best eaten fresh, but can be stored, tightly covered, in a cool place 2 or 3 days.

CINNAMON-SUGAR TWISTS
MAKES 14 TWISTS

1 **package (8 ounces) refrigerated crescent roll dough**

½ **cup coarse sugar**

1 **teaspoon ground cinnamon**

1 Unroll dough on work surface. Cut crosswise into 1-inch strips. Roll strips to form thin ropes; fold in half and twist halves together. Combine sugar and cinnamon in shallow dish.

2 Preheat air fryer to 370°F. Line basket with parchment paper; spray with nonstick cooking spray.

3 Cook in batches 6 to 8 minutes or until golden brown. Spray with cooking spray; roll in cinnamon-sugar mixture to coat. Serve warm.

CANDIED NUTS
MAKES ABOUT 3 CUPS

1 **egg white**	2 **tablespoons lemon juice**
1½ **cups whole almonds**	2 **teaspoons grated orange peel**
1½ **cups pecan halves**	1 **teaspoon grated lemon peel**
1 **cup powdered sugar**	⅛ **teaspoon ground nutmeg**

1 Beat egg white in medium bowl. Add almonds and pecans; stir until well coated. Combine powdered sugar, lemon juice, orange peel, lemon peel and nutmeg in medium bowl. Combine nuts and sugar mixture; toss until well coated.

2 Preheat air fryer to 300°F. Spray basket with nonstick cooking spray.

3 Cook 18 to 20 minutes, shaking several times during cooking. Cool slightly. Store in airtight container up to 2 weeks.

SAVORY PITA CHIPS
MAKES 4 SERVINGS

2 **whole wheat or white pita bread rounds**

3 **tablespoons grated Parmesan cheese**

1 **teaspoon dried basil**

¼ **teaspoon garlic powder**

1 Carefully cut each pita round in half horizontally; split into two rounds. Cut each round into six wedges. Spray wedges with nonstick cooking spray.

2 Combine Parmesan cheese, basil and garlic powder in small bowl; sprinkle evenly over pita wedges.

3 Preheat air fryer to 350°F.

4 Cook 8 to 10 minutes, shaking occasionally during cooking, until golden brown. Cool completely.

CINNAMON CRISPS

Substitute butter-flavored cooking spray for olive oil cooking spray and 1 tablespoon sugar mixed with ¼ teaspoon ground cinnamon for Parmesan cheese, basil and garlic powder.

BITE-YOU-BACK ROASTED EDAMAME

MAKES 4 SERVINGS

2 **teaspoons vegetable oil**

2 **teaspoons honey**

¼ **teaspoon wasabi powder***

1 **package (about 12 ounces) shelled edamame, thawed if frozen**

Kosher salt (optional)

*Wasabi powder can be found in the Asian section of most supermarkets and in Asian specialty markets.

1 Combine oil, honey and wasabi powder in large bowl; mix well. Add edamame; toss to coat.

2 Preheat air fryer to 370°F.

3 Cook 12 to 14 minutes, shaking occasionally during cooking, until lightly browned. Remove from basket to large bowl; sprinkle generously with salt, if desired. Cool completely before serving. Store in airtight container.

ROASTED CHICKPEAS
MAKES 1 CUP (4 SERVINGS)

1 **can (about 15 ounces) chickpeas, rinsed and drained**

2 **tablespoons olive oil**

½ **teaspoon salt**

½ **teaspoon black pepper**

½ **tablespoon chili powder**

¼ **teaspoon ground red pepper**

1 **lime, cut into wedges (optional)**

1 Combine chickpeas, oil, salt and black pepper in large bowl; toss to mix well.

2 Preheat air fryer to 390°F.

3 Cook 8 to 10 minutes, shaking occasionally during cooking, until chickpeas begin to brown.

4 Sprinkle with chili powder and ground red pepper. Serve with lime wedges, if desired.

EASY WONTON CHIPS
MAKES 2 DOZEN CHIPS (4 SERVINGS)

1½ **teaspoons soy sauce**

1 **teaspoon peanut or vegetable oil**

½ **teaspoon sugar**

¼ **teaspoon garlic salt**

12 **wonton wrappers**

1 Combine soy sauce, oil, sugar and garlic salt in small bowl; mix well.

2 Cut wonton wrappers diagonally in half. Spray with nonstick cooking spray. Brush soy sauce mixture lightly over both sides.

3 Preheat air fryer to 370°F. Cook in batches 3 to 5 minutes, shaking halfway through cooking, until crisp and lightly browned. Transfer to wire rack; cool completely.

BEET CHIPS
MAKES 2 TO 3 SERVINGS

3 **medium beets (red and/or golden), trimmed**
1½ **tablespoons extra virgin olive oil**

¼ **teaspoon salt**
¼ **teaspoon black pepper**

1 Cut beets into very thin slices, about ⅛ inch thick. Combine beets, oil, salt and pepper in medium bowl; gently toss to coat.

2 Preheat air fryer to 390°F.

3 Cook 15 to 18 minutes or until darkened and crisp. Cool completely.

EGGPLANT NIBBLES
MAKES 4 SERVINGS

1 **egg**
1 **tablespoon water**
½ **cup Italian-seasoned dry bread crumbs**

1 **Asian eggplant or 1 small globe eggplant**
Marinara sauce (optional)

1 Beat egg and water in shallow dish. Place bread crumbs in another shallow dish.

2 Cut ends off of eggplant. Cut into sticks about 3 inches long by ½-inch wide.

3 Coat eggplant sticks in egg, then roll in bread crumbs. Spray with olive oil cooking spray.

4 Preheat air fryer to 370°F. Line basket with foil or parchment paper.

5 Cook 12 to 14 minutes, shaking occasionally during cooking, until eggplant is tender and lightly browned. Serve with marinara sauce, if desired.

EASY ENTRÉES

BUTTERMILK AIR-FRIED CHICKEN
MAKES 4 SERVINGS

1 cut-up whole chicken (2½ to 3 pounds)
1 cup buttermilk
¾ cup all-purpose flour

½ teaspoon salt
½ teaspoon ground red pepper
¼ teaspoon garlic powder
2 cups plain dry bread crumbs

1 Place chicken pieces in large resealable food storage bag. Pour buttermilk over chicken. Close and refrigerate; let marinate at least 2 hours.

2 Preheat air fryer to 390°F. Spray basket with nonstick cooking spray.

3 Combine flour, salt, ground red pepper and garlic powder in large shallow bowl. Place bread crumbs in another shallow bowl.

4 Remove chicken pieces from buttermilk; coat with flour mixture then coat in bread crumbs. Spray chicken with cooking spray. Cook 20 to 25 minutes or until brown and crisp on all sides and cooked through (165°F). Serve warm.

COCONUT SHRIMP
MAKES 4 SERVINGS

DIPPING SAUCE

- ½ **cup orange marmalade**
- ⅓ **cup Thai chili sauce**
- 1 **teaspoon prepared horseradish**
- ½ **teaspoon salt**

SHRIMP

- 1 **cup flat beer**
- 1 **cup all-purpose flour**
- 2 **cups sweetened flaked coconut, divided**
- 2 **tablespoons sugar**
- 16 **to 20 large raw shrimp, peeled and deveined (with tails on), patted dry**

1 For dipping sauce, combine marmalade, chili sauce, horseradish and salt in small bowl; mix well. Cover and refrigerate until ready to serve.

2 For shrimp, whisk beer, flour, ½ cup coconut and sugar in large bowl until well blended. Place remaining 1½ cups coconut in medium bowl.

3 Preheat air fryer to 390°F. Line basket with parchment paper; spray with nonstick cooking spray.

4 Dip shrimp in beer batter, then in coconut, turning to coat completely. Cook in batches 5 to 7 minutes, turning halfway through cooking, until golden brown. Serve with dipping sauce.

PARMESAN-CRUSTED TILAPIA
MAKES 4 SERVINGS

⅔ **cup plus 3 tablespoons grated Parmesan cheese, divided**

⅔ **cup panko bread crumbs**

⅓ **cup prepared Alfredo sauce (refrigerated or jarred)**

1½ **teaspoons dried parsley flakes**

4 **tilapia fillets (6 ounces each)**

Shaved Parmesan cheese (optional)

Minced fresh parsley (optional)

1 Combine ⅔ cup grated cheese and panko in medium bowl; mix well. Combine Alfredo sauce, remaining 3 tablespoons grated cheese and parsley flakes in small bowl; mix well. Spread mixture over top of fish, coating in thick even layer. Top with panko mixture, pressing in gently to adhere.

2 Preheat air fryer to 390°F. Line basket with foil or parchment paper; spray with nonstick cooking spray.

3 Cook in batches 8 to 10 minutes or until crust is golden brown and fish begins to flake when tested with fork. Garnish with shaved Parmesan and fresh parsley.

CHICKEN AIR-FRIED STEAK WITH CREAMY GRAVY

MAKES 4 TO 6 SERVINGS

½ **cup all-purpose flour**

½ **teaspoon kosher salt**

½ **teaspoon onion powder**

¼ **teaspoon paprika**

¼ **teaspoon ground red pepper**

⅛ **teaspoon black pepper**

1 **large egg**

¼ **cup water**

1 **pound cube steak, divided into 4 to 6 portions**

GRAVY

1½ **tablespoons butter**

2 **to 3 tablespoons all-purpose flour**

¾ **cup chicken broth**

½ **cup milk**

Salt and black pepper

1 Combine ½ cup flour, kosher salt, onion powder, paprika, ground red pepper and black pepper in shallow dish. Whisk egg and water in another shallow dish.

2 Dredge steaks in flour mixture, then egg mixture, letting excess drain back into dish, then again in flour mixture to coat well.

3 Preheat air fryer to 370°F. Spray basket with nonstick cooking spray or line with parchment paper sprayed with cooking spray.

4 Cook in batches 12 to 14 minutes, turning and spraying with cooking spray halfway through cooking, until steaks are browned and no longer pink in middle. Remove to serving plate.

5 For gravy, melt butter in small skillet over medium heat. Add 2 tablespoons flour, broth and milk. Cook and stir until slightly thickened. If necessary, add additional 1 tablespoon flour to thicken. Season with salt and pepper. Serve steaks with gravy.

EASY AIR-FRIED CHICKEN THIGHS
MAKES 4 SERVINGS

8 **bone-in or boneless chicken thighs with skin**
1 **teaspoon garlic powder**
1 **teaspoon onion powder**
1 **teaspoon dried oregano**

1 **teaspoon ground thyme**
1 **teaspoon paprika**
1 **teaspoon salt**
1 **teaspoon black pepper**

1 Place chicken in large resealable food storage bag. Combine garlic powder, onion powder, oregano, thyme, paprika, salt and pepper in small bowl; mix well. Add to chicken; shake until spices are distributed.

2 Preheat air fryer to 350°F. Line basket with parchment paper; spray with nonstick cooking spray.

3 Cook in batches 20 to 25 minutes until golden browned and cooked throughout, turning chicken halfway through cooking.

NOTE

Try this chicken with other favorite spices as well.

SPICY SALMON
MAKES 4 SERVINGS

½ **teaspoon ground cumin**
½ **teaspoon chili powder**
½ **teaspoon salt**

¼ **teaspoon black pepper**
¼ **teaspoon paprika**
4 **salmon fillets (about 4 ounces each)**

1 Combine cumin, chili powder, salt, pepper and paprika in small bowl. Rub over top of salmon.

2 Preheat air fryer to 350°F. Line basket with parchment paper; spray with nonstick cooking spray.

3 Cook 8 to 10 minutes or until salmon is lightly crispy and easily flakes when tested with a fork.

SERVING SUGGESTION

Serve with tossed salad and rice.

CHICKEN WITH HERB STUFFING
MAKES 4 SERVINGS

⅓ **cup fresh basil leaves**

1 **package (8 ounces) goat cheese with garlic and herbs**

4 **boneless skinless chicken breasts**

1 **tablespoon olive oil**

1 Place basil in food processor; process using on/off pulsing action until chopped. Cut cheese into large pieces and add to food processor; process using on/off pulsing action until combined.

2 Place 1 chicken breast on cutting board and cover with plastic wrap. Pound with meat mallet until ¼ inch thick. Repeat with remaining chicken.

3 Shape about 2 tablespoons of cheese mixture into log and set in center of each chicken breast. Wrap chicken around filling to enclose completely. Tie securely with kitchen string. Drizzle with oil.

4 Preheat air fryer to 370°F. Cook 15 to 20 minutes or until chicken is cooked through and filling is hot. Allow to cool slightly, remove string and slice to serve.

SOUTHERN CRAB CAKES WITH RÉMOULADE DIPPING SAUCE

MAKES 8 SERVINGS

10 ounces fresh lump crabmeat

1½ cups fresh white or sourdough bread crumbs, divided

¼ cup chopped green onions

½ cup mayonnaise, divided

1 egg white, lightly beaten

2 tablespoons coarse grain or spicy brown mustard, divided

¾ teaspoon hot pepper sauce, divided

Lemon wedges (optional)

1 Pick out and discard any shell or cartilage from crabmeat. Combine crabmeat, ¾ cup bread crumbs and green onions in medium bowl. Add ¼ cup mayonnaise, egg white, 1 tablespoon mustard and ½ teaspoon hot pepper sauce; mix well. Using ¼ cup mixture per cake, shape into eight ½-inch-thick cakes. Roll crab cakes lightly in remaining ¾ cup bread crumbs.

2 Preheat air fryer to 370°F. Line basket with parchment paper.

3 Cook in batches 8 to 10 minutes, turning halfway through cooking, until golden brown.

4 For dipping sauce, combine remaining ¼ cup mayonnaise, 1 tablespoon mustard and ¼ teaspoon hot pepper sauce in small bowl; mix well.

5 Serve crab cakes with dipping sauce and lemon wedges, if desired.

CHICKEN BURGERS WITH WHITE CHEDDAR
MAKES 4 SERVINGS

1¼ **pounds ground chicken or turkey**

1 **cup plain dry bread crumbs**

½ **cup diced red bell pepper**

½ **cup ground walnuts**

¼ **cup sliced green onions**

¼ **cup light beer**

2 **tablespoons chopped fresh parsley**

2 **tablespoons lemon juice**

2 **cloves garlic, minced**

1 **teaspoon salt**

¼ **teaspoon black pepper**

4 **slices white Cheddar cheese**

4 **whole wheat buns**

Dijon mustard and lettuce leaves

1 Combine chicken, bread crumbs, bell pepper, walnuts, green onions, beer, parsley, lemon juice, garlic, salt and black pepper in large bowl; mix lightly. Shape into four patties.

2 Preheat air fryer to 390°F. Spray basket with nonstick cooking spray.

3 Cook 12 to 14 minutes, turning halfway through cooking, until burgers are cooked through. Place cheese on patties; cook 1 minute or just until cheese melts.

4 Serve burgers on buns with mustard and lettuce.

BLUE CHEESE STUFFED CHICKEN BREASTS
MAKES 4 SERVINGS

½ **cup crumbled blue cheese**

2 **tablespoons butter, softened, divided**

¾ **teaspoon dried thyme**

Salt and black pepper

4 **bone-in skin-on chicken breasts**

1 **tablespoon lemon juice**

1 Combine cheese, 1 tablespoon butter and thyme in small bowl; mix well. Season with salt and pepper.

2 Loosen chicken skin by pushing fingers between skin and meat, taking care not to tear skin. Spread cheese mixture under skin; massage skin to spread mixture evenly over chicken breast.

3 Melt remaining 1 tablespoon butter in small bowl; stir in lemon juice until blended. Brush mixture over chicken. Sprinkle with salt and pepper.

4 Preheat air fryer to 370°F. Cook 22 to 24 minutes or until chicken is cooked through.

BREADED VEAL SCALLOPINI WITH MUSHROOMS

MAKES 2 SERVINGS

½ **pound veal cutlets**

¼ **teaspoon salt**

⅛ **teaspoon black pepper**

1 **egg**

1 **tablespoon water**

½ **cup plain dry bread crumbs**

1 **tablespoon unsalted butter**

2 **large shallots, chopped (about ¼ cup)**

8 **ounces exotic mushrooms, such as cremini, oyster, baby bella and shiitake***

½ **teaspoon herbes de Provence****

½ **cup reduced-sodium chicken broth**

2 **lemon wedges (optional)**

Exotic mushrooms make this dish special. However, you can substitute white button mushrooms, if you prefer.

**Herbes de Provence is a mixture of basil, fennel, lavender, marjoram, rosemary, sage, savory and thyme used to season meat, poultry and vegetables.*

1 Season cutlets with salt and pepper. Lightly beat egg with water in shallow dish. Place bread crumbs in separate shallow dish.

2 Dip cutlet into egg, letting excess drip off. Dip in bread crumbs, turning to coat. Repeat with remaining cutlets.

3 Preheat air fryer to 370°F. Spray basket with nonstick cooking spray. Cook 12 to 15 minutes, turning halfway, until golden brown and cooked through. Transfer to plate.

4 Heat butter in large medium skillet over medium-high heat. Add shallots; cook and stir 1 to 2 minutes or until translucent. Add mushrooms and herbes de Provence; cook and stir 3 to 4 minutes or until most of liquid is evaporated. Stir in broth; cook 2 to 3 minutes or until slightly thickened.

5 Pour mushroom mixture over cutlets. Garnish with lemon wedges.

SALMON-POTATO CAKES WITH MUSTARD TARTAR SAUCE

MAKES 2 SERVINGS

3 small unpeeled red potatoes (8 ounces), halved

1 cup water

1 cup flaked cooked salmon

2 green onions, chopped

1 egg white

2 tablespoons chopped fresh parsley, divided

½ teaspoon Cajun or Creole seasoning

1 tablespoon mayonnaise

1 tablespoon plain fat-free yogurt or fat-free sour cream

2 teaspoons coarse grain mustard

1 tablespoon chopped dill pickle

1 teaspoon lemon juice

1 Place potatoes and water in medium saucepan. Bring to a boil. Reduce heat and simmer about 15 minutes or until potatoes are tender. Drain. Mash potatoes with fork, leaving chunky texture.

2 Combine mashed potatoes, salmon, green onions, egg white, 1 tablespoon parsley and Cajun seasoning in medium bowl.

3 Preheat air fryer to 370°F. Gently shape salmon mixture into two patties; flatten slightly. Cook 5 to 6 minutes, turning halfway through cooking, until browned and heated through.

4 Meanwhile, combine mayonnaise, yogurt, mustard, remaining 1 tablespoon parsley, pickle and lemon juice in small bowl. Serve sauce with cakes.

BIG KID SHRIMP

MAKES 4 SERVINGS

½ **cup plain dry bread crumbs**

¼ **cup grated Parmesan cheese**

½ **teaspoon paprika**

½ **teaspoon salt**

⅛ **teaspoon black pepper**

2 **tablespoons butter, melted**

1 **pound large raw shrimp, peeled and deveined (with tails on)**

½ **cup mayonnaise**

½ **cup ketchup**

1 **tablespoon sweet pickle relish**

1 Combine bread crumbs, Parmesan cheese, paprika, salt and pepper in large bowl. Add butter; mix well. Rinse shrimp under cold water, drain, and toss with bread crumb mixture.

2 Preheat air fryer to 390°F. Line basket with parchment paper; spray with nonstick cooking spray.

3 Cook 5 to 7 minutes or until lightly browned and cooked through.

4 Combine mayonnaise, ketchup and relish in small bowl. Serve with shrimp.

CHICKEN WITH KALE STUFFING
MAKES 4 SERVINGS

4 **boneless skinless chicken breasts**

1 **cup sliced mushrooms**

½ **cup chopped onion**

2 **tablespoons dry white wine**

1 **teaspoon chopped fresh oregano** *or* ¼ **teaspoon dried oregano**

1 **clove garlic, minced**

½ **teaspoon black pepper**

2 **cups packed chopped stemmed kale**

2 **tablespoons light mayonnaise**

½ **cup seasoned dry bread crumbs**

1 Pound chicken with meat mallet to ½-inch thickness; set aside.

2 Heat skillet over medium-high heat. Add mushrooms, onion, wine, oregano, garlic and pepper; cook and stir about 5 minutes or until onion is tender. Add kale; cook and stir until wilted.

3 Spread kale mixture evenly over flattened chicken breasts. Roll up chicken; secure with toothpicks. Brush chicken with mayonnaise; coat with bread crumbs.

4 Preheat air fryer to 370°F. Spray basket with nonstick cooking spray.

5 Cook chicken, seam sides down, 15 to 20 minutes or until golden brown and no longer pink in center. Remove toothpicks before serving.

FRIED BUTTERMILK CHICKEN FINGERS

MAKES 4 SERVINGS

CHICKEN

- 1½ **cups biscuit baking mix (regular, not low-fat)**
- 1 **cup buttermilk***
- 1 **egg, beaten**
- 12 **chicken tenders (about 1½ pounds), rinsed and patted dry**

DIPPING SAUCE

- ⅓ **cup mayonnaise**
- 1 **tablespoon honey**
- 1 **tablespoon prepared mustard**
- 1 **tablespoon packed dark brown sugar**

If you don't have buttermilk, substitute 1 tablespoon vinegar or lemon juice plus enough milk to equal 1 cup. Let stand 5 minutes.

1 Place biscuit mix in pie pan or shallow dish. Combine buttermilk and egg in another shallow dish; mix until well blended.

2 Roll chicken pieces in biscuit mix, one at a time, coating evenly on all sides. Dip each chicken piece in buttermilk mixture; roll in biscuit mix again to coat evenly.

3 Preheat air fryer to 390°F. Cook in batches 10 to 12 minutes or until golden.

4 For dipping sauce, combine mayonnaise, honey, mustard and brown sugar in small bowl. Serve with chicken.

BREADED PORK CUTLETS WITH TONKATSU SAUCE

MAKES 4 SERVINGS

Tonkatsu Sauce (recipe follows)

½ cup all-purpose flour

2 eggs, beaten with 2 tablespoons water

1½ cups panko bread crumbs

1 pound pork tenderloin, trimmed of fat and sliced into ½-inch-thick pieces

2 cups hot cooked rice

1 Prepare Tonkatsu Sauce; set aside.

2 Place flour in shallow dish. Place eggs in another shallow dish. Spread panko on medium plate. Dip each pork slice first in flour, then egg. Shake off excess and coat in panko.

3 Preheat air fryer to 370°F. Cook 12 to 15 minutes or until cooked through.

4 Serve over rice with Tonkatsu Sauce.

TONKATSU SAUCE

MAKES ABOUT ⅓ CUP SAUCE

¼ cup ketchup

1 tablespoon soy sauce

2 teaspoons sugar

2 teaspoons mirin (Japanese sweet rice wine)

1 teaspoon Worcestershire sauce

½ teaspoon grated fresh ginger

1 clove garlic, minced

Combine ketchup, soy sauce, sugar, mirin, Worcestershire sauce, ginger and garlic in small bowl.

FRIED TOFU WITH ASIAN VEGETABLES
MAKES 6 SERVINGS

1 pound firm tofu

¼ cup soy sauce, divided

1 cup all-purpose flour

⅛ teaspoon black pepper

1 package (16 ounces) frozen mixed Asian vegetables*

3 tablespoons water

1 teaspoon cornstarch

3 tablespoons plum sauce

2 tablespoons lemon juice

2 teaspoons sugar

1 teaspoon minced fresh ginger

⅛ to ¼ teaspoon red pepper flakes

Frozen vegetables do not need to be thawed before cooking.

1 Drain tofu; cut into ¾-inch cubes. Gently mix tofu and 2 tablespoons soy sauce in shallow dish; let stand 5 minutes. Combine flour and black pepper on plate. Gently toss tofu cubes, a small amount at a time, with flour mixture to coat. Spray tofu with nonstick cooking spray.

2 Preheat air fryer to 390°F. Cook in batches 3 to 4 minutes or until browned. Remove to plate; keep warm.

3 Place frozen vegetables in basket. Cook 3 to 4 minutes, shaking halfway through cooking, until vegetables are heated through. Set aside; cover to keep warm.

4 Stir water into cornstarch in small bowl until well blended. Combine cornstarch mixture, remaining 2 tablespoons soy sauce, plum sauce, lemon juice, sugar, ginger and red pepper flakes in medium microwavable bowl; cover and heat in microwave on HIGH 1 minute or until sauce is slightly thickened; stir to mix well. Spoon vegetables into serving bowl. Top with tofu and sauce; toss gently to mix.

BAKED PANKO CHICKEN
MAKES 2 SERVINGS

½ **cup panko bread crumbs**

3 **teaspoons assorted dried herbs (such as rosemary, basil, parsley, thyme or oregano), divided**

Salt and black pepper

2 **tablespoons mayonnaise**

2 **boneless skinless chicken breasts**

1 Combine panko, 1 teaspoon herbs, salt and pepper in shallow dish. Combine mayonnaise and remaining 2 teaspoons herbs in small bowl. Spread mayonnaise mixture onto chicken. Coat chicken with panko mixture, pressing to adhere.

2 Preheat air fryer to 390°F. Line basket with parchment paper; spray with nonstick cooking spray.

3 Cook 18 to 20 minutes or until chicken is browned and no longer pink in center.

FUN FOR KIDS

MOZZARELLA STICKS
MAKES 4 TO 6 SERVINGS

¼ cup all-purpose flour
2 eggs
1 tablespoon water
1 cup plain dry bread crumbs
2 teaspoons Italian seasoning
½ teaspoon salt

½ teaspoon garlic powder
1 package (12 ounces) string cheese (12 sticks)
1 cup marinara or pizza sauce, heated

1 Place flour in shallow dish. Whisk eggs and water in another shallow dish. Combine bread crumbs, Italian seasoning, salt and garlic powder in third shallow dish.

2 Coat each piece of cheese with flour. Dip in egg mixture, letting excess drip back into bowl. Roll in bread crumb mixture to coat. Dip again in egg mixture and roll again in bread crumb mixture. Refrigerate until ready to cook.

3 Preheat air fryer to 370°F. Line basket with parchment paper; spray with nonstick cooking spray.

4 Cook in batches 8 to 10 minutes, shaking halfway through cooking, until golden brown. Serve with marinara sauce.

MEATBALL MUMMIES
MAKES ABOUT 20 MUMMIES

1 **can (15 ounces) refrigerated crescent roll dough**
1 **package (20 ounces) frozen meatballs**

Black olive slices
1 **tablespoon marinara sauce, plus additional for dipping**

1 Unroll dough onto large cutting board. Press seams together; cut lengthwise into 20 strips. Wrap each meatball with one strip of dough, stretching dough to circle meatballs.

2 Dip olives into 1 tablespoon of marinara sauce. Place 2 olive slices on each meatball for eyes.

3 Preheat air fryer to 370°F. Line basket with parchment paper.

4 Cook in batches 8 to 10 minutes or until golden brown.

PIGGIES IN A BASKET
MAKES 4 SERVINGS

1 can (8 ounces) refrigerated crescent rolls

1 package (about 12 ounces) cocktail franks

1 Cut crescent dough into strips. Wrap dough around each frank.

2 Preheat air fryer to 350°F.

3 Cook in batches 3 to 4 minutes or until golden brown.

CRISPY RANCH CHICKEN BITES
MAKES 4 SERVINGS

1 pound boneless skinless chicken breasts

¾ cup ranch dressing, plus additional for serving

2 cups panko bread crumbs

1 Cut chicken into 1-inch cubes. Place ¾ cup dressing in small bowl. Spread panko in shallow dish. Dip chicken in dressing; shake off excess. Roll in panko to coat. Spray chicken with nonstick cooking spray.

2 Preheat air fryer to 370°F. Line basket with parchment paper.

3 Cook in batches 8 to 10 minutes or until golden brown and cooked through. Serve with additional ranch dressing.

CANDY CALZONE
MAKES 16 SERVINGS

1 package small chocolate, peanut and nougat candy bars, chocolate peanut butter cups or other chocolate candy bar (8 bars)

1 package (about 15 ounces) refrigerated pie crusts (2 crusts)

½ cup milk chocolate chips

1 Chop candy into ¼-inch pieces.

2 Unroll pie crusts on cutting board or clean surface. Cut out 3-inch circles with biscuit cutter. Place about 1 tablespoon chopped candy on one side of each circle; fold dough over candy to form semicircle. Crimp edges with fingers or fork to seal.

3 Preheat air fryer to 370°F. Line basket with parchment paper. Cook in batches 8 to 10 minutes or until golden brown. Remove to wire rack to cool slightly.

4 Place chocolate chips in small microwavable bowl; microwave on HIGH 1 minute. Stir; microwave in 30-second intervals, stirring until smooth. Drizzle melted chocolate over calzones; serve warm.

CHICKEN CORNDOG BITES
MAKES 16 BITES

1 **package (8 ounces) refrigerated dough sheet**

1 **package (9 ounces) Italian-seasoned cooked chicken breast strips**

Mustard

Ketchup

1 Unroll dough on lightly floured surface. Roll into 12×9-inch rectangle; cut into 16 (4×3-inch) pieces.

2 Cut chicken strips in half crosswise. Place one piece of chicken on each piece of dough; wrap dough around chicken and seal, pressing edges together tightly.

3 Preheat air fryer to 370°F. Line basket with parchment paper or foil.

4 Cook in batches 5 to 7 minutes or until light golden brown. Decorate with mustard and ketchup. Serve warm with additional mustard and ketchup for dipping.

SANDWICH MONSTERS
MAKES 7 SERVINGS

1 package (about 16 ounces) refrigerated jumbo buttermilk biscuit dough (8 biscuits)

1 cup (4 ounces) shredded mozzarella cheese

⅓ cup sliced mushrooms

2 ounces pepperoni slices (about 35 slices), quartered

½ cup pizza sauce, plus additional for dipping

1 egg, beaten

1 Separate biscuits; set aside one biscuit for decorations. Roll out remaining biscuits into 7-inch circles on lightly floured surface.

2 Top half of each circle evenly with cheese, mushrooms, pepperoni and sauce, leaving ½-inch border. Fold dough over filling to form semicircle; seal edges with fork. Brush tops with egg.

3 Split remaining biscuit horizontally; cut each half into eight ¼-inch strips. For each sandwich, roll two strips of dough into spirals to create eyes. Divide remaining two strips of dough into seven pieces to create noses. Arrange eyes and noses on tops of sandwiches; brush with egg.

4 Preheat air fryer to 370°F. Line basket with parchment paper or foil.

5 Cook in batches 6 to 8 minutes or until golden brown. Remove to wire rack; cool 5 minutes. Serve with additional pizza sauce.

TIP

Don't worry about leaking sauce or cheese—it will look like it's coming from the monster's mouth!

MINI CHEESE DOGS
MAKES 32 MINI CHEESE DOGS

1 package (16 ounces) hot dogs (8 hot dogs)

6 ounces pasteurized process cheese product

2 packages (16 ounces each) jumbo homestyle refrigerated buttermilk biscuit dough (8 biscuits per package)

1 Preheat air fryer to 370°F. Line basket with parchment paper or spray with nonstick cooking spray.

2 Cut each hot dog into four pieces. Cut cheese into 32 (1×½-inch) pieces.

3 Separate biscuits; cut each biscuit in half. Wrap one piece of hot dog and one piece of cheese in each piece of dough.

4 Cook 5 to 7 minutes or until biscuits are golden brown. Serve warm.

VEGGIE VARIATION

To make this snack vegetarian-friendly, substitute 8 veggie dogs (soy protein links) for the regular hot dogs. Veggie dogs can be found in the produce section and sometimes the freezer section of the supermarket.

SPEEDY SALAMI SPIRALS
MAKES ABOUT 28 SPIRALS

1 package (about 14 ounces) refrigerated pizza dough

1 cup (4 ounces) shredded Italian cheese blend

3 to 4 ounces thinly sliced Genoa salami

1 Unroll dough on cutting board or clean work surface; press into 15×10-inch rectangle. Sprinkle evenly with cheese; top with salami.

2 Starting with long side, tightly roll up dough and filling jelly-roll style, pinching seam to seal. Cut roll crosswise into ½-inch slices. (If roll is too soft to cut, refrigerate or freeze until firm.)

3 Preheat air fryer to 390°F. Line basket with parchment paper.

4 Cook in batches 8 to 10 minutes or until golden brown. Serve warm.

FOXY FACE FOLDOVERS

MAKES 18 PASTRIES

1 **ripe medium banana**

1 **package (17¼ ounces) frozen puff pastry sheets (2 sheets), thawed according to package directions**

9 **tablespoons semisweet chocolate chips, divided**

36 **sliced almonds**

18 **dried sweetened cranberries**

1 Peel banana and place in resealable food storage bag; seal. Squeeze banana into a pulp.

2 Place puff pastry sheets on lightly floured surface. Cut each sheet into nine even squares.

3 Place 1 teaspoon chocolate chips in center of each square. Cut small corner off one end of banana-filled bag. Squeeze about ½ teaspoon banana pulp over chocolate chips.

4 Fold each puff pastry square into a triangle by bringing opposing corners together; press edges together with tines of fork to seal.

5 Preheat air fryer to 370°F. Cook in batches 8 to 10 minutes until crispy and golden brown. Remove to wire racks to cool completely.

6 When pastries are cool, place remaining 6 tablespoons chocolate chips in small resealable food storage bag. Microwave on HIGH 30 seconds or until melted. Cut small corner off one end of bag; use melted chocolate to create ears and whiskers and to attach almonds and cranberries for eyes and noses.

PORKY PINWHEELS
MAKES 24 PINWHEELS

1 **sheet frozen puff pastry (half of 17¼-ounce package), thawed**

1 **egg white, beaten**

8 **slices bacon, crisp-cooked and crumbled**

2 **tablespoons packed brown sugar**

¼ **teaspoon ground red pepper**

1 Place pastry on sheet of parchment paper. Brush with egg white.

2 Combine bacon, brown sugar and ground red pepper in small bowl. Sprinkle evenly over top of pastry; press lightly to adhere. Roll pastry jelly-roll style from long end. Wrap in parchment paper. Refrigerate 30 minutes.

3 Preheat air fryer to 370°F. Line basket with parchment paper. Slice pastry into ½-inch-thick slices.

4 Cook in batches 8 to 10 minutes or until light golden brown. Remove to wire racks; cool completely.

BITE-SIZED S'MORES
MAKES 20 S'MORES

40 wonton wrappers

2 whole graham crackers, each broken into 10 small pieces

40 mini marshmallows

⅓ cup large chunk chocolate chips

6 tablespoons plus 2 teaspoons raspberry jam

1 egg, beaten

Powdered sugar

1 Place 20 wonton wrappers on counter. Keep remaining wonton wrappers covered with damp cloth. Place one piece graham cracker in center of each wonton. Top with 2 marshmallows, 2 chocolate chunk chips and 1 teaspoon raspberry jam.

2 Brush edges of wonton wrapper with egg. Top with plain wonton, pressing edges to seal. Gently fold or crimp wonton to curl up edges. Repeat with remaining wontons. Cover with plastic wrap until ready to cook.

3 Preheat air fryer to 370°F. Line basket with parchment paper.

4 Cook in batches 5 to 7 minutes or until lightly browned. Remove carefully from air fryer; cool slightly. Sprinkle with powdered sugar.

CINNAMON TOAST POPPERS
MAKES 12 SERVINGS

6 **cups fresh bread* cubes (1-inch cubes)**

2 **tablespoons butter, melted**

1 **tablespoon plus 1½ teaspoons sugar**

½ **teaspoon ground cinnamon**

Use a firm sourdough, whole wheat or semolina bread.

1 Place bread cubes in large bowl. Drizzle with butter; toss to coat.

2 Combine sugar and cinnamon in small bowl. Sprinkle over bread cubes; mix well.

3 Preheat air fryer to 350°F. Cook 10 to 12 minutes, shaking occasionally during cooking, until bread is golden and fragrant. Serve warm or at room temperature.

CHOCOLATE-PEANUT BUTTER BANANAS
MAKES 2 SERVINGS

¼ cup chocolate syrup

1 tablespoon peanut butter

1 large firm banana, unpeeled

1 teaspoon melted butter

1 tablespoon packed brown sugar

1 cup vanilla ice cream

2 tablespoons chopped peanuts

1 Place chocolate syrup in small bowl; microwave on HIGH 10 to 15 seconds until warm. Slowly whisk in peanut butter until well blended. Keep warm until ready to serve.

2 Preheat air fryer to 350°F. Line basket with foil or parchment paper. Cut unpeeled banana in half lengthwise. Brush cut sides with butter; place cut side down in basket. Cook 1½ to 2 minutes. Turn banana; spread brown sugar over banana. Cook 1 to 2 minutes or until brown sugar melts and banana softens.

3 Peel banana; cut each piece in half. Place two pieces in each serving dish. Top with ice cream. Drizzle with warm chocolate sauce; sprinkle with peanuts.

NOTE

To chop peanuts, place in small resealable food storage bag and crush slightly with a meat mallet.

GRILLED CHEESE KABOBS
MAKES 12 SERVINGS

8 thick slices whole wheat bread

3 thick slices sharp Cheddar cheese

3 thick slices Monterey Jack or Colby Jack cheese

2 tablespoons butter, melted

1 Cut each slice bread into 1-inch squares. Cut each slice cheese into 1-inch squares. Make small sandwiches with one square of bread and one square of each type of cheese. Top with second square of bread. Brush sandwiches with butter.

2 Preheat air fryer to 370°F. Cook sandwich squares 30 seconds to 1 minute until golden brown and cheese is slightly melted.

3 Place sandwiches on the ends of short wooden skewers, if desired, or eat as finger food.

SUGAR-AND-SPICE TWISTS
MAKES 12 SERVINGS

2 tablespoons granulated sugar
½ teaspoon ground cinnamon

1 package (about 11 ounces) refrigerated breadstick dough (12 breadsticks)

1 Combine sugar and cinnamon in shallow dish or plate. Separate breadsticks; roll each piece into 12-inch rope. Roll ropes in sugar-cinnamon mixture to coat. Twist each rope into pretzel shape.

2 Preheat air fryer to 370°F. Line basket with parchment paper; spray with nonstick cooking spray.

3 Cook in batches 8 to 10 minutes or until lightly browned. Remove to wire rack to cool 5 minutes. Serve warm.

HINT

Use colored sugar sprinkles in place of the granulated sugar in this recipe for a fun "twist" of color perfect for holidays, birthdays or simple everyday celebrations.

FRIED CHICKEN FINGERS WITH DIPPING SAUCE

MAKES 4 SERVINGS

¼ **cup plain yogurt**

2 **tablespoons honey**

2 **tablespoons prepared mustard**

2 **teaspoons cider vinegar**

1 **tablespoon sugar**

¼ **teaspoon ground cinnamon**

1 **teaspoon paprika**

½ **teaspoon garlic powder**

½ **teaspoon salt, divided**

¼ **teaspoon black pepper**

1½ **cups panko bread crumbs**

⅓ **cup buttermilk**

2 **egg whites**

8 **chicken tenders (about 1¼ pounds)**

1 For dipping sauce, combine yogurt, honey, mustard, vinegar, sugar and cinnamon in small bowl; set aside.

2 Combine paprika, garlic powder, ¼ teaspoon salt and black pepper in small bowl; set aside. Place panko in shallow dish. Whisk buttermilk and egg whites in medium bowl. Add chicken to buttermilk mixture; toss until well coated.

3 Coat chicken with panko, one piece at a time, pressing down lightly to adhere. Sprinkle chicken evenly with paprika mixture.

4 Preheat air fryer to 390°F. Line basket with parchment paper.

5 Cook in batches 10 to 12 minutes or until chicken is golden brown and crispy and no longer pink in center.

6 Sprinkle chicken with remaining ¼ teaspoon salt, if desired. Serve with sauce.

APPLE AND CHEESE POCKETS
MAKES 8 SERVINGS

2 cups Golden Delicious apples, peeled, cored and finely chopped (about 2 medium)

2 cups (8 ounces) shredded sharp Cheddar cheese

2 tablespoons apple jelly

¼ teaspoon curry powder

1 package (about 16 ounces) large refrigerated biscuit dough (8 biscuits)

1 Combine apples, cheese, jelly and curry powder in large bowl; stir well.

2 Flatten each biscuit on lightly floured surface to 6½-inch circle. Place ½ cup apple mixture in center. Fold over filling to form semicircle; press to seal tightly. Repeat with remaining biscuits and filling.

3 Preheat air fryer to 370°F. Line basket with parchment paper. Cook in batches 8 to 10 minutes or until biscuits are golden and filling is heated through.

TIPS

Refrigerate leftovers up to 2 days or freeze up to 1 month.

To reheat thawed pockets, microwave about 30 seconds on HIGH or until heated through.

SIDE KICKS

BUTTERNUT SQUASH FRIES
MAKES 4 SERVINGS

½ teaspoon garlic powder

¼ teaspoon salt

¼ teaspoon ground red pepper

1 butternut squash (about
   2½ pounds), peeled, seeded
   and cut into 2-inch-thin slices

2 teaspoons vegetable oil

1 Combine garlic powder, salt and ground red pepper in small bowl; set aside.

2 Place squash in large bowl. Drizzle with oil and sprinkle with seasoning mix; gently toss to coat.

3 Preheat air fryer to 390°F. Cook in batches 16 to 18 minutes, shaking halfway during cooking, until squash is tender and begins to brown.

PESTO-PARMESAN TWISTS
MAKES 24 BREADSTICKS

1 package (about 11 ounces) refrigerated bread dough

All-purpose flour

¼ cup prepared pesto

⅔ cup grated Parmesan cheese, divided

1 tablespoon olive oil

1 Roll out dough into 20×10-inch rectangle on lightly floured surface. Spread pesto evenly over half of dough; sprinkle with ⅓ cup Parmesan cheese. Fold remaining half of dough over filling, forming 10-inch square.

2 Cut into 12 (1-inch) strips with sharp knife. Cut strips in half crosswise to form 24 strips total. Twist each strip several times.

3 Brush breadsticks with oil; sprinkle with remaining ⅓ cup Parmesan cheese.

4 Preheat air fryer to 370°F. Cook in batches 8 to 10 minutes or until golden brown. Serve warm.

GARLIC ROASTED OLIVES AND TOMATOES
MAKES ABOUT 2 CUPS

1 **cup assorted olives, pitted**
1 **cup grape tomatoes, halved**
4 **cloves garlic, sliced**

1 **tablespoon olive oil**
1 **tablespoon herbes de Provence**

1 Pat olives dry with paper towels.

2 Combine olives, tomatoes, garlic and oil in small bowl. Toss with herbes de Provence; mix well.

3 Preheat air fryer to 370°F. Cook 5 to 7 minutes until browned and blistered, shaking occasionally during cooking. Remove to bowl.

SERVING SUGGESTION

Try tossing this with hot cooked pasta for a main dish.

AIR-FRIED CORN-ON-THE-COB
MAKES 2 SERVINGS

2 teaspoons butter, melted

¼ teaspoon salt

½ teaspoon black pepper

½ teaspoon chopped fresh parsley

2 ears corn, husks and silks removed

Foil

Grated Parmesan cheese (optional)

1 Combine butter, salt, pepper and parsley in small bowl. Brush corn with butter mixture. Wrap each ear of corn in foil.*

2 Preheat air fryer to 390°F. Cook 10 to 12 minutes, turning halfway through cooking. Sprinkle with cheese before serving, if desired.

*If your air fryer basket is on the smaller side, you may need to break ears of corn in half to fit.

CRISPY FRIES WITH HERBED DIPPING SAUCE

MAKES 3 SERVINGS

**Herbed Dipping Sauce
(recipe follows)**
2 large unpeeled baking potatoes

1 tablespoon vegetable oil
½ teaspoon kosher salt

1 Prepare Herbed Dipping Sauce; set aside.

2 Cut potatoes into ¼-inch strips. Toss potato strips with oil in large bowl to coat evenly.

3 Preheat air fryer to 390°F. Spray basket with nonstick cooking spray.

4 Cook in batches 18 to 20 minutes, shaking occasionally during cooking, until golden brown and crispy. Sprinkle with salt. Serve immediately with Herbed Dipping Sauce.

HERBED DIPPING SAUCE

Stir ¼ cup mayonnaise, 1 tablespoon chopped fresh herbs (such as basil, parsley, oregano and/or dill), ¼ teaspoon salt and ⅛ teaspoon black pepper in small bowl until smooth and well blended. Cover and refrigerate until ready to serve.

FRIED CAULIFLOWER FLORETS
MAKES 4 SERVINGS

1 **head cauliflower**
1 **tablespoon olive oil**
½ **teaspoon salt**
¼ **teaspoon ground black pepper**

½ **teaspoon chopped fresh parsley**
3 **tablespoons grated Parmesan cheese**
2 **tablespoons panko bread crumbs**

1 Cut cauliflower into florets. Place in large bowl. Drizzle with oil. Sprinkle with salt, pepper and parsley.

2 Preheat air fryer to 390°F. Spray basket with nonstick cooking spray.

3 Cook in batches 6 to 8 minutes until golden brown and slightly tender, shaking halfway through cooking.

4 Combine cheese and panko in small bowl. Sprinkle over top of cauliflower. Cook 2 to 3 minutes or until browned.

GARLIC KNOTS
MAKES 20 KNOTS

4 tablespoons (½ stick) butter, divided

1 tablespoon olive oil

1 tablespoon minced garlic

½ teaspoon salt

¼ teaspoon garlic powder

1 package (11 ounces) refrigerated bread dough

½ cup grated Parmesan cheese

2 tablespoons chopped fresh parsley

½ teaspoon dried oregano

1 Melt 2 tablespoons butter in small saucepan over low heat. Add oil, garlic, salt and garlic powder; cook over very low heat 5 minutes. Pour into small bowl; set aside.

2 Roll out dough into 8×10-inch rectangle. Cut into 20 squares. Roll each piece into 8-inch rope; tie in a knot. Brush knots with garlic mixture.

3 Preheat air fryer to 370°F. Line basket with parchment paper.

4 Cook in batches 8 to 10 minutes or until knots are lightly browned. Meanwhile, melt remaining 2 tablespoons butter. Combine cheese, parsley and oregano in small bowl; mix well. Brush melted butter over warm knots; immediately sprinkle with Parmesan cheese mixture. Cool slightly; serve warm.

PARMESAN POTATO WEDGES
MAKES 6 SERVINGS

2 pounds unpeeled red potatoes
2 tablespoons butter, melted
1½ teaspoons dried oregano
½ teaspoon salt

Black pepper
2 tablespoons grated Parmesan cheese

1 Boil potatoes in salted water 8 to 10 minutes or until fork-tender. Drain. Cool completely.

2 Cut cooled potatoes into wedges; place in large bowl. Add butter, oregano, salt and pepper; mix gently.

3 Preheat air fryer to 390°F. Line basket with parchment paper.

4 Cook potatoes 8 to 10 minutes, shaking occasionally during cooking, until golden brown and crispy. Place in large bowl; toss with Parmesan cheese.

ZUCCHINI FRITTE
MAKES 4 SERVINGS

Lemon Aioli (recipe follows)

¾ to 1 cup soda water

½ cup all-purpose flour

¼ cup cornstarch

½ teaspoon coarse salt, plus additional for serving

¼ teaspoon garlic powder

¼ teaspoon dried oregano

¼ teaspoon black pepper

3 cups panko bread crumbs

1½ pounds medium zucchini (about 8 inches long), ends trimmed, cut lengthwise into ¼-inch-thick slices

¼ cup grated Parmesan or Romano cheese

Chopped fresh parsley

Lemon wedges

1 Prepare Lemon Aioli; cover and refrigerate until ready to use.

2 Pour ¾ cup soda water into large bowl. Combine flour, cornstarch, ½ teaspoon salt, garlic powder, oregano and pepper in medium bowl; mix well. Gradually whisk flour mixture into soda water just until blended. Add additional soda water, if necessary, to reach consistency of thin pancake batter. Place panko in shallow dish.

3 Working with one at a time, dip zucchini slices into batter to coat; let excess batter drip back into bowl. Add to panko; pressing into zucchini slices to coat both sides completely.

4 Preheat air fryer to 390°F.

5 Cook in batches 7 to 10 minutes or until golden brown. Sprinkle with cheese and parsley. Serve with Lemon Aioli and lemon wedges.

LEMON AIOLI

Combine ½ cup mayonnaise, 2 tablespoons lemon juice, 1 tablespoon chopped fresh Italian parsley and 1 clove minced garlic in small bowl; mix well. Season with salt and pepper.

SWEET POTATO FRIES
MAKES 2 SERVINGS

2 sweet potatoes, peeled
and sliced

1 tablespoon olive oil

¼ teaspoon coarse salt

¼ teaspoon black pepper

½ cup grated Parmesan cheese
(optional)

1 Toss potatoes with oil, salt and pepper in medium bowl.

2 Preheat air fryer to 390°F. Spray basket with nonstick cooking spray.

3 Cook 10 to 12 minutes, shaking occasionally during cooking, until lightly browned. Sprinkle with cheese, if desired.

GREEN BEAN FRIES
MAKES 6 SERVINGS

DIPPING SAUCE

- ½ **cup light mayonnaise**
- ¼ **cup light sour cream**
- ¼ **cup low-fat buttermilk**
- ¼ **cup minced peeled cucumber**
- 1½ **teaspoons lemon juice**
- 1 **clove garlic**
- 1 **teaspoon wasabi powder**
- 1 **teaspoon prepared horseradish**
- ½ **teaspoon dried dill weed**
- ½ **teaspoon dried parsley flakes**
- ½ **teaspoon salt**
- ⅛ **teaspoon ground red pepper**

GREEN BEAN FRIES

- 8 **ounces fresh green beans, trimmed**
- ⅓ **cup all-purpose flour**
- ⅓ **cup cornstarch**
- ½ **cup reduced-fat (2%) milk**
- 1 **egg**
- ¾ **cup plain dry bread crumbs**
- 1 **teaspoon salt**
- ½ **teaspoon onion powder**
- ¼ **teaspoon garlic powder**

1 For dipping sauce, combine mayonnaise, sour cream, buttermilk, cucumber, lemon juice, garlic, wasabi powder, horseradish, dill weed, parsley flakes, salt and ground red pepper in blender; blend until smooth. Refrigerate until ready to use.

2 For green bean fries, bring large saucepan of salted water to a boil. Add green beans; cook 4 minutes or until crisp-tender. Drain and run under cold running water to stop cooking.

3 Combine flour and cornstarch in large bowl. Whisk milk and egg in another large bowl. Combine bread crumbs, salt, onion powder and garlic powder in shallow dish. Place green beans in flour mixture; toss to coat. Working in batches, coat beans with egg mixture, letting excess drain back into bowl. Roll green beans in bread crumb mixture to coat.

4 Preheat air fryer to 390°F. Cook in batches 6 to 8 minutes, shaking occasionally during cooking, until golden brown. Serve warm with dipping sauce.

FRIED GREEN TOMATOES
MAKES 4 SERVINGS

⅓ cup all-purpose flour

¼ teaspoon salt

2 eggs

1 tablespoon water

½ cup panko bread crumbs

2 large green tomatoes, cut into ½-inch-thick slices

½ cup ranch dressing

1 tablespoon sriracha sauce

1 package (5 ounces) spring greens salad mix

¼ cup crumbled goat cheese

1 Combine flour and salt in shallow dish. Beat eggs and water in another shallow dish. Place panko in third shallow dish. Coat tomato slices with flour, shaking off excess. Dip in egg mixture, letting excess drip back into bowl. Roll in panko to coat. Place on plate.

2 Preheat air fryer to 390°F. Line basket with parchment paper.

3 Cook in batches 6 to 8 minutes or until golden brown.

4 Combine ranch dressing and sriracha in small bowl; mix well. Divide greens among four serving plates; top with tomatoes. Drizzle with dressing mixture; sprinkle with cheese.

BACON-ROASTED BRUSSELS SPROUTS
MAKES 4 SERVINGS

1 pound Brussels sprouts

3 slices bacon, cut into ½-inch pieces

2 teaspoons packed brown sugar

Salt and black pepper

1 Trim ends from Brussels sprouts; cut in half lengthwise.

2 Combine Brussels sprouts, bacon and brown sugar in large bowl.

3 Preheat air fryer to 390°F. Cook 15 to 18 minutes, shaking occasionally during cooking, until golden brown. Season with salt and pepper.

CAPRESE PORTOBELLOS
MAKES 4 SERVINGS

2 tablespoons butter

½ teaspoon minced garlic

1 teaspoon dried parsley flakes

4 portobello mushrooms, stems removed

1 cup (4 ounces) shredded mozzarella cheese

1 cup cherry or grape tomatoes, thinly sliced

2 tablespoons fresh basil, thinly sliced

Balsamic glaze

1 Combine butter, garlic and parsley flakes in small dish. Microwave on LOW 30 seconds until melted.

2 Wash mushrooms thoroughly; dry on paper towels. Brush both sides of mushrooms with butter mixture.

3 Preheat air fryer to 390°F. Spray basket with nonstick cooking spray.

4 Fill mushroom caps with about ¼ cup cheese each. Top with sliced tomatoes. Cook 5 to 7 minutes or until cheese is melted and lightly browned. Top with basil.

5 Drizzle with balsamic glaze before serving.

CURLY AIR-FRIED FRIES
MAKES 4 SERVINGS

2 **large russet potatoes, unpeeled**
¼ **cup finely chopped onion**
1 **teaspoon vegetable oil**
½ **teaspoon salt**

¼ **teaspoon black pepper**
Honey mustard dipping sauce, ketchup or other favorite dipping sauce

1 Spiral potatoes with thick spiral blade of spiralizer.*

2 Place potatoes and onion in large bowl; drizzle with oil. Toss well.

3 Preheat air fryer to 390°F. Line basket with parchment paper. Cook 12 to 15 minutes or until golden brown and crispy, shaking occasionally during cooking. Sprinkle with salt and pepper.

4 Serve with dipping sauce.

If you do not have a spiralizer, cut potatoes into thin strips.

ORANGE GLAZED CARROTS
MAKES 6 SERVINGS

1 **package (32 ounces) baby carrots**
1 **tablespoon packed light brown sugar**
1 **tablespoon orange juice**

1 **tablespoon melted butter**
¼ **teaspoon ground cinnamon**
⅛ **teaspoon ground nutmeg**
Orange peel and fresh chopped parsley (optional)

1 Place carrots in large bowl. Combine brown sugar, orange juice and butter in small bowl. Pour over carrots; toss well.

2 Preheat air fryer to 390°F.

3 Cook 6 to 8 minutes, shaking occasionally during cooking, until carrots are tender and lightly browned. Remove to serving dish. Sprinkle with cinnamon and nutmeg. Garnish with orange peel and parsley.

KALE CHIPS
MAKES 6 SERVINGS

1 **large bunch kale (about 1 pound)**
1 **tablespoon olive oil**
1 **teaspoon garlic powder**

½ **teaspoon salt**
½ **teaspoon black pepper**

1 Wash kale and pat dry with paper towels. Remove center ribs and stems; discard. Cut leaves into 2- to 3-inch-wide pieces.

2 Combine leaves, oil, garlic powder, salt and pepper in large bowl; toss to coat.

3 Preheat air fryer to 390°F.

4 Cook in batches 3 to 4 minutes or until edges are lightly browned and leaves are crisp. Cool completely. Store in airtight container.

ORANGE AND MAPLE-GLAZED ROASTED BEETS
MAKES 4 SERVINGS

4 **medium beets, scrubbed**

¼ **cup orange juice**

3 **tablespoons balsamic or cider vinegar**

2 **tablespoons maple syrup**

2 **teaspoons grated orange peel, divided**

1 **teaspoon Dijon mustard**

Salt and black pepper

1 **to 2 tablespoons chopped fresh mint (optional)**

1 Peel and cut beets in half lengthwise; cut into wedges. Place in large bowl.

2 Whisk orange juice, vinegar, maple syrup, 1 teaspoon orange peel and mustard in small bowl until well blended. Pour half over beets.

3 Preheat air fryer to 390°F.

4 Cook 22 to 25 minutes, shaking occasionally during cooking, until softened. Remove to serving dish; pour remaining orange juice mixture over beets. Season with salt and pepper. Sprinkle with remaining 1 teaspoon orange peel and mint, if desired.

SERVING SUGGESTION

The flavors of this recipe make it a great side dish to serve at your holiday meal.

OVEN "FRIES"
MAKES 2 SERVINGS

2 **small russet potatoes
   (10 ounces), refrigerated**

2 **teaspoons olive oil**
¼ **teaspoon salt or onion salt**

1 Peel potatoes and cut lengthwise into ¼-inch strips. Place in colander; rinse under cold running water 2 minutes. Drain. Pat dry with paper towels.

2 Preheat air fryer to 390°F. Meanwhile, place potatoes in large resealable food storage bag. Drizzle with oil. Seal bag; shake to coat evenly.

3 Cook 15 to 18 minutes, shaking occasionally during cooking, until light brown and crisp. Sprinkle with salt.

NOTE

Refrigerating potatoes—usually not recommended for storage—converts the starch in the potatoes to sugar, which enhances the browning when the potatoes are baked. Do not refrigerate the potatoes longer than 2 days, because they may develop a sweet flavor.

SWEET ENDINGS

FRIED PINEAPPLE WITH TOASTED COCONUT
MAKES 8 SERVINGS

1 large pineapple, cored and cut into chunks

½ cup packed brown sugar

1 teaspoon ground cinnamon

½ teaspoon ground nutmeg

½ cup toasted coconut*

Ice cream or whipped cream (optional)

Chopped macadamia nuts (optional)

*To toast the coconut in the air fryer, place coconut in small ramekin. Cook in preheated air fryer at 350°F for 2 to 3 minutes or until lightly browned.

1 Place pineapple chunks in large bowl. Combine brown sugar, cinnamon and nutmeg in small bowl; sprinkle over pineapple. Toss well. Refrigerate 30 minutes.

2 Preheat air fryer to 370°F. Spray basket with nonstick cooking spray.

3 Cook 6 to 8 minutes or until pineapple is browned and lightly crispy. Sprinkle with coconut. Serve with ice cream or macadamia nuts, if desired.

MIXED BERRY DESSERT LAVASH WITH HONEYED MASCARPONE
MAKES 4 SERVINGS

1½ cups assorted mixed fresh berries

2 tablespoons honey, divided

½ teaspoon vanilla

1 piece lavash bread, 7½ × 9½ inches

1 tablespoon melted butter

4 ounces (½ cup) mascarpone cheese

1 tablespoon julienned fresh mint leaves

1 Place berries in medium bowl; stir in 1 tablespoon honey and vanilla. Refrigerate until ready to use.

2 Brush both sides of lavash with butter; cut into four even pieces.

3 Preheat air fryer to 370°F. Line basket with parchment paper. Cook 6 to 8 minutes, turning halfway through cooking, until lavash is golden and crisp. Cool 5 minutes on wire rack.

4 Stir mascarpone and remaining 1 tablespoon honey in small bowl. Spread over each piece of lavash. Top with sweetened berries. Sprinkle with mint to serve.

TOASTED POUND CAKE
WITH BERRIES AND CREAM
MAKES 4 SERVINGS

1 frozen pound cake, thawed

2 tablespoons melted butter

1 cup fresh blackberries or blueberries

1 cup fresh raspberries or strawberries

Whipped topping, vanilla ice cream or prepared lemon curd

1 Cut pound cake into eight slices. Brush both sides of cake with butter.

2 Preheat air fryer to 370°F. Cook in batches 5 to 7 minutes, turning halfway through cooking, until cake is lightly browned.

3 Serve with fresh berries, whipped topping or lemon curd, as desired.

UPSIDE-DOWN APPLES
MAKES 2 SERVINGS

Foil

2 tablespoons finely chopped pecans or walnuts

2 tablespoons chopped dried apricots or any dried fruit

¼ teaspoon ground cinnamon

¼ teaspoon vanilla

⅛ teaspoon ground nutmeg

⅛ teaspoon salt

1 tablespoon honey or maple syrup

1 Fuji apple (about 8 ounces), halved and cored

½ cup vanilla ice cream

1 Cut two 12×12-inch pieces foil; spray with nonstick cooking spray.

2 Combine pecans, apricots, cinnamon, vanilla, nutmeg and salt in small bowl; mix well. Spread over foil. Drizzle with honey. Place apple halves on top of nut mixture, cut side down. Wrap foil around apple.

3 Preheat air fryer to 370°F. Cook 20 to 22 minutes or just until tender. Serve apple and nut mixture with ice cream.

TIP

Fuji apples are a combination of Red Delicious and Ralls Janet apples. They are crisp and juicy apples that hold their shape when baking. If Fuji apples are not available, substitute Braeburn or Gala apples.

APPLE PIE POCKETS
MAKES 4 SERVINGS

2 pieces lavash bread, each cut into 4 rectangles

2 tablespoons melted butter

¾ cup apple pie filling

1 egg, lightly beaten with 1 teaspoon water

½ cup powdered sugar

⅛ teaspoon ground cinnamon

2½ teaspoons milk

1 Brush one side of each piece of lavash with butter. Place half of the pieces, buttered-side down, on work surface. Spoon 3 tablespoons pie filling in center of each lavash, leaving ½-inch border uncovered. Using pastry brush, brush border with egg wash. Top with remaining lavash pieces, buttered-side up. Using tines of fork, press edges together to seal. Use paring knife to cut three small slits in center of each pie pocket.

2 Preheat air fryer to 370°F. Line basket with parchment paper.

3 Cook in batches 8 to 10 minutes or until crust is golden and crisp. Remove to wire rack; cool 15 minutes.

4 Combine powdered sugar, cinnamon and milk in small bowl; whisk until smooth. Drizzle over pockets; let stand 15 minutes to allow glaze to slightly set.

DOUGHNUT HOLE FONDUE
MAKES 5 SERVINGS

1 can (about 6 ounces) refrigerated biscuit dough (5 biscuits)

3 tablespoons butter, divided

1 tablespoon sugar

¼ teaspoon ground cinnamon

¾ cup whipping cream

1 cup bittersweet or semisweet chocolate chips

½ teaspoon vanilla

Sliced fresh fruit, such as pineapple, strawberries and cantaloupe

1 Separate biscuits into five portions. Cut each in half; roll dough into balls to create 10 balls.

2 Place 2 tablespoons butter in small microwavable bowl. Microwave 30 seconds until melted; stir. Combine sugar and cinnamon in small dish. Dip balls in melted butter; roll in cinnamon-sugar mixture.

3 Preheat air fryer to 370°F. Spray basket with nonstick cooking spray.

4 Cook in batches 4 to 5 minutes or until golden brown.

5 Meanwhile, heat cream in small saucepan until bubbles form around edge. Remove from heat. Add chocolate; let stand 2 minutes or until softened. Add remaining 1 tablespoon butter and vanilla; whisk until smooth. Keep warm in fondue pot or transfer to serving bowl.

6 Serve with doughnut holes and fruit.

CHOCOLATE-COFFEE NAPOLEONS
MAKES 6 NAPOLEONS

1 tablespoon instant coffee granules

¼ cup warm water

1 package (4-serving size) chocolate instant pudding and pie filling mix

1¾ cups whole milk plus 1 teaspoon whole milk, divided

1 sheet frozen puff pastry (half of 17¼-ounce package), thawed

3 tablespoons powdered sugar

2 tablespoons bittersweet or semisweet chocolate chips

1 Dissolve coffee in water in small bowl; set aside to cool.

2 Combine pudding mix, 1¾ cups milk and coffee in medium bowl; mix according to package directions. Cover and refrigerate until needed.

3 Preheat air fryer to 370°F. Unfold pastry sheet; cut into three strips along fold marks. Cut each strip crosswise into thirds, forming nine squares total. Cook in batches 8 to 10 minutes or until puffed and golden brown. Remove to wire rack to cool completely.

4 Blend powdered sugar and remaining 1 teaspoon milk in small bowl until smooth. Cut each pastry square in half crosswise with serrated knife to form 18 pieces total. Spread powdered sugar icing over tops of six pastry pieces.

5 Place chocolate chips in small resealable food storage bag. Microwave on MEDIUM (50%) 30 seconds or until melted. Cut small piece off one corner of bag; drizzle over iced pastry pieces. Place in refrigerator while assembling napoleons.

6 Spoon about 2 tablespoons pudding mixture over each of six pastry pieces; layer with remaining six pastry pieces and pudding mixture. Top with iced pastry pieces. Refrigerate until ready to serve.

PLUM-GINGER BRUSCHETTA
MAKES 9 SERVINGS

1 **sheet frozen puff pastry (half of 17¼-ounce package), thawed**

2 **cups chopped unpeeled firm ripe plums (about 3 medium)**

2 **tablespoons sugar**

2 **tablespoons chopped candied ginger**

1 **tablespoon all-purpose flour**

2 **teaspoons lemon juice**

⅛ **teaspoon ground cinnamon**

2 **tablespoons apple jelly *or* apricot preserves**

1 Cut puff pastry sheet lengthwise into three strips. Cut each strip crosswise in thirds to make nine pieces.

2 Preheat air fryer to 370°F. Line basket with parchment paper. Cook in batches 5 to 6 minutes or until puffed and lightly browned.

3 Meanwhile, combine plums, sugar, ginger, flour, lemon juice and cinnamon in medium bowl.

4 Gently brush each puff pastry piece with about ½ teaspoon jelly; top with scant ¼ cup plum mixture. Cook in batches 1 to 2 minutes or until fruit is tender.

FRUIT TARTS
MAKES 2 SERVINGS

1 refrigerated pie crust (half of a 15-ounce package)

1 tablespoon melted butter

¼ cup apple, cherry or blueberry pie filling

Coarse sugar

1 Unroll pie crust on clean work surface; cut into four pieces. Brush butter over dough. Spread pie filling over two pieces of dough; top each with second piece of dough. Seal edges by crimping with tines of a fork. Brush tops with butter; sprinkle with sugar.

2 Preheat air fryer to 370°F. Line basket with parchment paper.

3 Cook 6 to 8 minutes or until light golden brown. Remove to plate; cool.

CHOCOLATE ROLLS

MAKES 16 ROLLS

8 tablespoons granulated sugar, divided

1 package (about 15 ounces) refrigerated pie crusts (2 crusts)

1 cup semisweet chocolate chips

1 egg white, beaten

Powdered sugar (optional)

1 Sprinkle 2 tablespoons granulated sugar on cutting board or work surface. Roll out one pie crust over sugar. Sprinkle pie crust with 2 tablespoons granulated sugar. Using pizza wheel or sharp knife, trim away 1 inch dough from four sides to form square. (Save dough trimmings for another use or discard.)

2 Cut square in half; cut each half crosswise into four pieces to form eight small (4×2-inch) rectangles. Place heaping teaspoon chocolate chips at one short end of each rectangle; roll up, enclosing chocolate chips. Brush lightly with egg white. Repeat with remaining crust.

3 Preheat air fryer to 370°F. Spray basket with nonstick cooking spray.

4 Cook in batches 8 to 10 minutes or until lightly browned. Cool 10 minutes to serve warm, or cool completely. Sprinkle with powdered sugar, if desired.

ROASTED PLUMS
WITH SPICED TOPPING
MAKES 4 SERVINGS

¼ **cup toasted walnuts,* chopped**

⅛ **teaspoon ground cumin**

⅛ **teaspoon ground cinnamon**

1 **teaspoon ground ginger**

4 **red plums, pitted and cut in half**

1 **teaspoon olive oil**

¼ **cup crumbled Gorgonzola cheese**

*To toast nuts, cook in preheated 350°F parchment-lined air fryer 3 to 4 minutes until golden brown.

1 Preheat air fryer to 350°F. Line basket with parchment paper.

2 Combine walnuts, cumin, cinnamon and ginger in small bowl; set aside.

3 Brush plums with oil. Cook, cut sides up, 6 to 8 minutes or until tender. Remove plums to serving plate.

4 Sprinkle with cheese and walnuts.

BACON S'MORES BUNDLES
MAKES 4 SERVINGS

1¼ cups mini marshmallows

¾ cup semisweet chocolate chips

¾ cup coarsely crushed graham crackers (5 whole graham crackers)

4 slices bacon, crisp-cooked and crumbled

1 package (17¼ ounces) frozen puff pastry (2 sheets), thawed

All-purpose flour

1 Combine marshmallows, chocolate chips, graham crackers and bacon in medium bowl.

2 Unfold pastry on lightly floured surface. Roll each pastry sheet into 12-inch square; cut into four 6-inch squares. Place scant ½ cup marshmallow mixture in center of each square.

3 Brush edges of pastry squares with water. Bring edges together over filling; twist tightly to seal.

4 Preheat air fryer to 370°F. Cook in batches 6 to 8 minutes or until golden brown. Remove to wire rack; cool 5 minutes. Serve warm.

CHERRY TURNOVERS
MAKES 12 TURNOVERS

1 **can (21 ounces) cherry pie filling**
2 **teaspoons grated orange peel**
1 **package (about 15 ounces) refrigerated pie crusts (2 crusts)**

1 **egg yolk**
1 **tablespoon milk**
1 **tablespoon sugar**
½ **teaspoon ground cinnamon**

1 Combine pie filling and orange peel in medium bowl.

2 Roll out one pie crust into 12-inch circle on lightly floured surface. Cut out six 4-inch circles with cookie cutter. Repeat with second crust.

3 Beat egg yolk and milk in small bowl until blended. Combine sugar and cinnamon in separate small bowl.

4 Spoon scant tablespoon pie filling mixture in center of each pastry circle. Brush edges of circles with egg yolk mixture; fold in half to enclose filling. Press edges together with fork to seal.

5 Cut slits in tops of turnovers with paring knife. Brush with remaining egg yolk mixture; sprinkle with cinnamon-sugar.

6 Preheat air fryer to 370°F. Cook in batches 8 to 10 minutes or until golden brown. Remove to wire rack; cool slightly. Serve warm.

PEACHES WITH RASPBERRY SAUCE
MAKES 4 SERVINGS

1 package (10 ounces) frozen raspberries, thawed

1½ teaspoons lemon juice

2 tablespoons packed brown sugar

½ teaspoon ground cinnamon

1 can (15 ounces) peach halves in juice (4 halves)

Foil

2 teaspoons butter, cut into small pieces

Fresh mint sprigs (optional)

1 Combine raspberries and lemon juice in food processor fitted with metal blade; process until smooth. Refrigerate until ready to serve.

2 Preheat air fryer to 350°F.

3 Combine brown sugar and cinnamon in medium bowl; coat peach halves with mixture. Place peach halves, cut sides up, on foil. Dot with butter. Fold foil over peaches. Place packet in basket.

4 Cook 6 to 8 minutes or until peaches are soft and lightly browned.

5 To serve, spoon 2 tablespoons raspberry sauce over each peach half. Garnish with mint.

SAUTÉED APPLES SUPREME

MAKES 2 SERVINGS

2 small Granny Smith apples *or* 1 large Granny Smith apple

1 teaspoon butter, melted

2 tablespoons unsweetened apple juice or cider

1 teaspoon packed brown sugar

½ teaspoon ground cinnamon

⅔ cup vanilla ice cream or frozen yogurt (optional)

2 tablespoons chopped walnuts, toasted*

*To toast nuts, cook in preheated 350°F parchment-lined air fryer 3 to 4 minutes until golden brown.

1 Cut apples into quarters; remove cores and cut into ½-inch-thick slices. Toss butter and apples in medium bowl.

2 Combine apple juice, brown sugar and cinnamon in small bowl; toss with apples.

3 Preheat air fryer to 350°F. Line basket with parchment paper; spray with nonstick cooking spray.

4 Cook 6 to 8 minutes, shaking halfway through cooking, until soft and lightly golden. Transfer to serving bowls; serve with ice cream, if desired. Sprinkle with walnuts.

BANANA BOWTIES
MAKES 20 BOWTIES

1 **cup peeled chopped ripe banana (about 2 medium)**

¼ **cup finely chopped walnuts or pecans**

1 **tablespoon packed brown sugar**

20 **square wonton wrappers**

1 **egg, beaten**

Chocolate syrup

1 Combine banana, nuts and brown sugar in small bowl; gently mix.

2 Arrange wonton wrappers, one at a time, on clean surface. Brush edges with egg. Place teaspoonful of banana filling in center. Fold wrapper in half, pressing edges to seal. Pinch center to form bowtie. Cover with plastic wrap and refrigerate until needed. Repeat with remaining wrappers and filling.

3 Preheat air fryer to 370°F.

4 Cook in batches 6 to 8 minutes or until golden brown. Drizzle with chocolate syrup. Serve immediately.

AIR-FRIED S'MORES
MAKES 2 SERVINGS

2 whole graham crackers,
  broken in half
  Foil
2 marshmallows

1 package (1.5 ounces) milk
  chocolate candy bar, broken
  in half

1 Preheat air fryer to 370°F. Place two graham cracker squares on two sheets of foil. Top each with marshmallows. Gather foil around graham crackers.

2 Place foil packets in basket. Cook 1½ to 2 minutes or until marshmallows are browned.

3 Remove carefully from basket. Top marshmallows with chocolate bar halves and remaining graham cracker squares. Bring sides together to create sandwich.

INDEX

INDEX

INDEX

INDEX

METRIC CONVERSION CHART

VOLUME MEASUREMENTS (dry)

1/8 teaspoon = 0.5 mL
1/4 teaspoon = 1 mL
1/2 teaspoon = 2 mL
3/4 teaspoon = 4 mL
1 teaspoon = 5 mL
1 tablespoon = 15 mL
2 tablespoons = 30 mL
1/4 cup = 60 mL
1/3 cup = 75 mL
1/2 cup = 125 mL
2/3 cup = 150 mL
3/4 cup = 175 mL
1 cup = 250 mL
2 cups = 1 pint = 500 mL
3 cups = 750 mL
4 cups = 1 quart = 1 L

VOLUME MEASUREMENTS (fluid)

1 fluid ounce (2 tablespoons) = 30 mL
4 fluid ounces (1/2 cup) = 125 mL
8 fluid ounces (1 cup) = 250 mL
12 fluid ounces (1 1/2 cups) = 375 mL
16 fluid ounces (2 cups) = 500 mL

WEIGHTS (mass)

1/2 ounce = 15 g
1 ounce = 30 g
3 ounces = 90 g
4 ounces = 120 g
8 ounces = 225 g
10 ounces = 285 g
12 ounces = 360 g
16 ounces = 1 pound = 450 g

DIMENSIONS

1/16 inch = 2 mm
1/8 inch = 3 mm
1/4 inch = 6 mm
1/2 inch = 1.5 cm
3/4 inch = 2 cm
1 inch = 2.5 cm

OVEN TEMPERATURES

250°F = 120°C
275°F = 140°C
300°F = 150°C
325°F = 160°C
350°F = 180°C
375°F = 190°C
400°F = 200°C
425°F = 220°C
450°F = 230°C

BAKING PAN SIZES

Utensil	Size in Inches/Quarts	Metric Volume	Size in Centimeters
Baking or Cake Pan (square or rectangular)	8×8×2	2 L	20×20×5
	9×9×2	2.5 L	23×23×5
	12×8×2	3 L	30×20×5
	13×9×2	3.5 L	33×23×5
Loaf Pan	8×4×3	1.5 L	20×10×7
	9×5×3	2 L	23×13×7
Round Layer Cake Pan	8×1½	1.2 L	20×4
	9×1½	1.5 L	23×4
Pie Plate	8×1¼	750 mL	20×3
	9×1¼	1 L	23×3
Baking Dish or Casserole	1 quart	1 L	—
	1½ quart	1.5 L	—
	2 quart	2 L	—